BEHIND THE HEADLINES

JOHN RUSSELL

HOJOPRESS PUBLISHING

This is a work of fiction. Names, characters, places, and incidents either are the product of the author's imagination or are used fictitiously. Any resemblance to actual persons, living or dead, events, or locales is entirely coincidental.

Copyright© 2025 by John Russell

All rights reserved. No part of this book may be reproduced or used in any manner without written permission of the copyright owner except for the use of quotations in a book review. For more information, address: info@hojopresspublishing.com

ISBN: 979-8-9923636-1-6

(paperback)

Book design by : Get Covers.com

www.hojopresspublishing.com

To Breanna,

Your hard work, kindness, and determination are a constant source of inspiration. Like the character in these pages, you manage to balance so many things with grace, always finding a way forward. Watching you grow and face life's challenges reminds me that even in the busy moments, there is always room for love, loyalty, and perseverance. This book is dedicated to you, for all the little things you do that make such a big difference. Thank you for being you.

Preface

In *Beyond the Headlines*, Breanna Robert's journey unfolds against challenges many of us recognize. The story weaves together the quiet struggles of balancing personal and professional responsibilities, uncovering hidden layers of power and corruption, and discovering the depth of resilience and loyalty that can carry us through even the toughest times.

As Breanna navigates the complexities of her career as an investigative journalist and her role as a wife, the theme of personal and professional conflict subtly resonates with the tension many of us face between our careers and personal lives. Finding a balance between competing responsibilities, whether managing expectations at work or maintaining meaningful relationships, can feel like a delicate dance. For Breanna, Ashley Moore, a driven and ambitious new co-anchor, adds an unexpected layer of complexity, reminding us that, in the real world, change often comes when we least expect it. The struggle to focus on our values, even as circumstances shift, is a challenge we all understand in our work and personal lives.

As the story unfolds, the undercurrents of power and corruption surface, reflecting the often unseen forces shaping our lives. Breanna's investigation into her town's political machinations reveals that systems of power, whether in politics, business, or even our personal lives, can be corrupt. The question of how far we should go to expose the truth, or the costs of standing up against those in power, is one that we've all grappled with. Our choices about transparency and accountability in our workplaces or communities influence our lives and the broader world.

Resilience and loyalty emerge as quiet yet powerful forces that carry Breanna through her journey. Breanna and Ashley reveal the quiet strength that helps them endure moments of doubt or hardship. Whether facing illness or fighting for justice, the characters' determination reflects an aspect of human nature that many of us recognize. We all encounter moments where resilience is required, whether in our struggles or in the relationships we hold dear. Loyalty, too, plays a subtle role—whether it's to family, friends, or our principles reminding us of the deep connections that bind us and give us the strength to press on.

Beyond the Headlines doesn't just tell a story about a journalist uncovering corruption. It explores themes woven into daily life's fabric. We all face moments of personal conflict, encounter power dynamics that shape our choices, and find resilience in the support of those we trust. These themes are universal, and in exploring them, the story reflects the quiet, often unnoticed forces that guide us through the complexities of our own lives.

Contents

Chapter 1	1
Chapter 2	11
Chapter 3	19
Chapter 4	31
Chapter 5	41
Chapter 6	53
Chapter 7	61
Chapter 8	71
Chapter 9	85
Chapter 10	99
Chapter 11	121
Acknowledgements	129
About the author	131

CHAPTER 1

The newsroom conference room at KBNR was a burst of color and excitement. Streamers in shades of gold and silver hung from the ceiling, and balloons floated above, adding a festive touch. Fresh flowers in vibrant hues filled every available vase, infusing the air with a hint of spring. I darted around, checking and rechecking details. John Gould my co-anchor for three years was now retiring and his retirement party had to be perfect.

"Breanna, where should we put the centerpieces?" Jenna, a staffer, asked, holding a stack of floral arrangements.

"Place them on the tables," I replied. "Make sure they're spaced. We need everything balanced."

I moved to the catering table next, scanning the food trays. My heart sank when I spotted pasta instead of the hors d'oeuvres I had selected. I dialed the company's number, my fingers trembling.

"Hello, this is Breanna from Channel 4. We received the wrong order for John's retirement celebration."

The voice on the other end was apologetic. "Let me check the order." After a while, he came back. "You are right. We'll send the correct items right away."

I focused on the retirement party with the caters working on the mix-up. Peers were gathering, chatting, and laughing as they set up chairs. I double-checked the projector to confirm that the surprise video was queued and ready.

"Breanna, everything is wonderful," said Mike, one of our senior reporters. "You've outdone yourself."

"Thanks. I want John Gloush, my co-anchor for 3 years, to have a memorable send-off," I replied, glancing around to check if everything was in place.

John walked in and looked around, smiling from ear to ear. His words hung in the air, a subtle hint of what would come.

I smiled, trying to push away the unease. "I hope you enjoy the party."

I returned to my tasks, the party's success riding on every detail. Despite the vibrant setting and upbeat atmosphere, I couldn't help but feel sad over John's retirement.

All the years, we worked together....

I thought my emotions would be in my control. But they weren't.

The conference room buzzed with staff mingling and chatting. I glanced at the faces of coworkers who had come together to celebrate his retirement. John looked both surprised and delighted, waving to everyone with a grin.

It was time to start this party. I looked around the room, checking that everything was in place. The staff had filled the room, and the buzz of banter grew louder. Laughter and clinking glasses filled the air as friends caught up and enjoyed the food at the tables.

I took a moment to gather my thoughts. With the catering mistake resolved, there were finally hors d'oeuvres, instead of pasta, on the table. And the decorations were in place, too.

Everything was ready, at last.

Jenna joined us, holding a glass of punch. "The video is going to be a hit. I watched the preview. You've got everyone talking."

I nodded, appreciating the support. "I hope so. It's hard to believe he's saying goodbye."

The room quieted, and I reached the podium, clutching my notes. My heart raced with each step. Coworkers settled into their seats, their chatter tapering off. All eyes on me; people waiting for my speech. I took a deep breath to calm myself.

"John," I said, my voice steady but warm, "you've been more than a mentor to us all. Your dedication and wisdom have guided us through countless struggles. Your contributions have shaped not our careers but our lives."

I paused, my stare sweeping across the room. "You've taught us the true meaning of integrity and perseverance. We'll miss your calm demeanor and ability to lead with strength and kindness. You've been a cornerstone of this broadcasting station, and it won't be the same without you."

A few nods. Some quiet sniffles. And several glasses raised in silent cheers.

I could see the emotions in John's eyes as he tried to hide them behind a tight smile. He stepped up to the podium, exhaling like he could steady himself at the moment alone.

A beat of silence.

Then he spoke. "Thank you. It's been an honor to work with such a dedicated staff. I admire each of you for your hard work and commitment. You've faced deadlines, breaking news, and long hours with unwavering resolve."

His glance shifted to me, and he smiled. "Breanna, I have immense respect for you. Your leadership, dedication, and passion for journalism have been a guiding force for us all. You've handled every challenge with grace and determination. I know you'll continue to inspire and lead this crew to even greater heights."

I swallowed hard, trying to keep my emotions in check. Hearing John's praise was both uplifting and bittersweet. Yet, I wasn't sure if the newsroom will ever feel the same. With John retiring and leaving behind many colleagues. And those who look up to him.

As he concluded his speech, he raised his glass. "To this incredible staff and Breanna, who will lead with the same integrity and passion. Here's to new beginnings and to face whatever comes with the same strength we've shown together."

The room echoed with applause and cheers. And I, too, raised my glass in a toast. Laughter and music filled the air as people mingled and enjoyed the party.

I spotted John in the crowd, surrounded by peers sharing stories and wishes. Joy filled his face, but an unfamiliar figure entering drew my attention.

And the energy in the room shifted.

A new face. A woman---tall, confident. Dark brown hair spilling over her shoulders, blue eyes scanning the space like she was already taking it in, filing it away. She moved with the quiet confidence of someone who knew exactly where she belonged.

Introductions followed. Ashley Moore, the new co-anchor.

She greeted the team with firm handshakes and friendly remarks, leaving a powerful impression with her charm and self-assurance.

Yet, something about her stuck with me.

I wasn't sure why.

Not yet.

I tried to stay out of the way as she made her rounds. She moved around, her laughter ringing above the rest. Her poised interactions and sharp, enthusiastic demeanor caught my eye.

"Breanna, have you met Ashley Moore?" Jenna asked, coming up beside me.

"Not yet," I replied, my eyes still following her. "I'm just taking it all in."

Ashley approached our group, her smile broad and her energy palpable. "Hi, I'm Ashley. I've heard so much about you."

Her confidence was obvious, and she made people relaxed.

A subtle unease settled in my chest. With her understandable ambition, people saw her eagerness to connect with everyone as almost calculated. I couldn't help but sense a hint of competition.

I forced a smile and joined the conversation. "Welcome. I'm Breanna."

Ashley's eyes met mine, and she extended her hand. "I'm looking forward to working with you."

Her handshake was firm, and her gaze steady. A spark in her eyes spoke with determination and implied a pang of uncertainty. This new dynamic has entered the mix.

While the party continued, I kept a watchful eye on her. She pulled focus as she interacted with her new colleges, effortlessly and enthusiastically. And that sparked a quiet sense of competition with me.

I slipped into a quieter corner to get away and to collect my thoughts.

Then, Ashley found me. She smiled as she joined me. "Breanna, mind if I steal you?"

I tried to keep my smile genuine. "Of course. What's up?"

She leaned against a nearby table, her posture relaxed but confident. "I've been looking forward to getting to meet everyone. This place got quite a reputation for being top-notch."

"Yeah, it's an outstanding team," I said, glancing around. "John's built something here."

She nodded. "I've heard a lot about what's next. Big changes. Exciting times."

Her tone was casual, but an edge to her cadence caught my interest. "Changes?"

"Oh, absolutely. I've got some ideas for the show. New formats, fresh angles. With them, I think, we can make an impact."

I tried to hide my apprehension. "That sounds ambitious. Change can be good."

Ashley's smile widened, almost as if she was testing my reaction. "I'm all about pushing boundaries. And I want to make sure that we're not just keeping up but *leading* the way."

The nature of her words masked an underlying determination. I sensed a subtle prickle of unease. Her ambition was clear; others saw her eagerness to start change as a direct challenge.

"Right," I said, meeting her gaze. "That should be interesting."

Her look lingered on me for a moment before she straightened up. "I'm sure we'll handle things together. I'm looking forward to working with you."

She walked away.

A moment later, I noticed her mingle with the other guests.

There it was. Beneath all that charm and energy, there was an edge. A quiet, calculated drive. And I wasn't sure if I liked it.

As the party continued, I wondered where my husband was. The conference room entrance buzzed with people leaving for home; the party's energy dying. It was then that I spotted my husband, Aaron, in the entrance hall. Finally, he's here.

I called out his name, waving him over. "I'm so glad you could make it."

He smiled and pulled me into an embrace. "I wouldn't miss it."

Ashley's spotting us, moved to greet us. "Hi there." Her eyes brightened and her voice carried a note of cheerful enthusiasm as she approached. "I'm Ashley Moore, and you are?."

He extended his hand, his expression polite. "My name is Aaron Roberts"

She shook his hand with one of her business smiles. "What do you do?"

"I'm a local veterinarian. And I'm here to pick up Breanna."

Ashley looked at him a moment more than necessary. "That's wonderful. I've always admired people who work in the community. It must be rewarding."

He agreed. "It's been a fulfilling career."

Ashley was almost too social. "I'm sure we'll have plenty of opportunities to chat."

I couldn't help but notice that she leaned in a little closer, and the way her eyes sparkled. Her eyeing Aron. These, I didn't like. Not at all.

While Aaron nodded at her, unaware of all the signs. "I'm looking forward to it."

But I didn't want to create a scene, so I tried to mask my discomfort as I turned back to Aaron. "I'm glad you're here."

The once-bustling atmosphere had now mellowed into a soft hum of chatter and the clinking of glasses. Empty plates, half-drunk flutes of champagne, and a few stray streamers still hanging from the ceiling filled the room, remnants of the party.

While Aron went off to grab some drinks, I spotted John gathered with his closest coworkers near the makeshift lounge area. And I joined the small circle of friends and familiar faces, all of whom had been part of John's journey, surrounding him. John expressed his gratitude to us all. "Thank you all for making this night memorable. I'm touched."

I stepped closer, my heart heavy with the reality of his departure. "You've meant so much to us. It's difficult to imagine this place without you."

He placed a hand on my shoulder; his look was warm and reassuring. "Breanna, you've been a rock for this team. You've got the passion and the heart to lead them through whatever comes next."

I swallowed hard, trying to keep my emotions in check. "I just hope I can do half as well as you did."

John's eyes held a hint of mischief as he smiled. "Remember, it's not about doing things the way I did. It's about staying true to your principles. Challenges will come, and they'll test you. You'll handle them just fine if you stay grounded and honest."

His words resonated. The future appeared both exciting and daunting. I understood the changes ahead would bring their ethical dilemmas. His advice about remaining genuine to oneself echoed as a promise and a warning.

"Thanks, John," I said. "Your guidance means a lot. I'll keep it in mind."

He gave me a final, heartfelt hug. "You'll do outstanding. I do not doubt that."

The room emptied. I lingered for a moment, watching him say goodbyes. The farewell settled over me like a shroud.

The evening's quiet gave me space to reflect. The newsroom's outlook was uncertain, and the new dynamics with Ashley were unfolding. Looking around at the remnants of the party. With a deep breath, I turned toward the exit, ready to face whatever lay ahead.

Aaron and I walked through the lit parking lot, and the cool night air was a welcome contrast to the crowded warmth of the studio. The traces of the celebration and the unsettling interaction with Ashley still lingered in my thoughts.

Aaron took my hand. His touch was a comforting presence. "John's farewell was memorable."

"Thanks," I said, squeezing his hand. "I'm glad it went well. There's something about tonight I can't shake."

He tilted his head, looking at me with concern. "What's on your mind?"

I hesitated, glancing back at the newsroom. "It's Ashley. She's so ambitious. I can't help but feel like she will shake things up around here. It caught my eye too. She's got plans."

"There's something else. Her interest in you seemed... a bit too much."

Aaron's eyebrows lifted in surprise. "Really? I didn't realize it."

"I'm probably overthinking it. It seems like she's trying to make a mark."

He paused, his expression thoughtful. "I understand your concern, but everyone brings their energy to a new role."

We drove from the studio—the car's quiet contrasted with the evening's buzz. Opportunities unfolded in ways I hadn't expected, and difficulties and opportunities lay ahead.

Chapter 2

It was Ashley's first day at the studio at KBNR. Ashley stood in the center of a small group, animatedly discussing her vision for the press room. Although colorful posters and notices about upcoming news segments adorned the walls, she dominated the space.

"Imagine if we could overhaul the whole segment lineup," she said, her voice ringing clear over the chatter. "We could introduce new, dynamic content that grabs viewers' attention."

She suggested modernizing the studio using the latest technology and changing our interview methods. The surrounding group was engaged, nodding in agreement.

"I've been thinking about how we could bring in more interactive elements. Engaging with viewers in real time could set us apart."

One of the senior reporters, Mark, hunched in. "That sounds ambitious. Do you have a timeline for these changes?"

Ashley smiled, a glint of something unreadable in her eyes. "I'm aiming for a full rollout by the end of the quarter. We must stay ahead of the curve to keep our upper hand."

Ashley's enthusiasm was infectious. Yet I sensed an underlying strategy behind her bold proposals. Like a prelude to a larger agenda.

The journalism office had settled into a lull, the clatter of keyboards and ringing phones fading as the day wound down. Soft, golden light filtered through the large windows, casting long shadows across the desks. The air carried the faint scent of coffee, now cold, abandoned in forgotten mugs. I tried focusing on the report before me.

She had made her arrival known. It was clear she was not here to do her job. I knew I needed to stay vigilant. Whatever her plans were, I had to be ready.

I sat at my desk, the weak light from my lamp cutting through the growing shadows. The office had quieted, with most of my colleagues gone for the night. I couldn't bring myself to go. Not yet.

I stared at the mess on top of my desk. Papers and phone messages needed my attention, but my beliefs were stuck on Ashley. She carried herself with a confidence that unnerved me, as if she knew something the rest of us didn't.

The door creaked open, and I heard footsteps approaching. I saw Rachel, my mentor, pausing by my desk. Her smile was warm, but laced with concern.

"Late night?" she asked, glancing at the papers scattered across my workspace.

"Yeah. Trying to get a handle on things."

She leaned against the border of my desk, her company comforted. "You've been quiet today, Breanna. Something on your mind?"

I hesitated, then sighed. "It's Ashley. There's... something about her."

She raised an eyebrow. "Something like?"

"She's ambitious. She talks about a change like it's inevitable. Like she's already planning her next moves."

Rachel nodded, her expression thoughtful. "Ambition isn't a bad thing, you know."

"I know. It's more than that. She's... strategic. How she interacts with everyone feels like she's figuring out how to move the pieces around."

"Aaron? Is she sizing him up, too?"

"I think so. She was with him earlier today, talking and laughing. It was more than casual conversation. There was something... calculated about it."

She didn't respond right away, letting the silence settle between us. "You're worried."

I nodded, sensing the words as I spoke them. "I don't want to be, but yes. I've worked hard to get where I am. I don't want to lose everything because someone else is more... strategic."

Rachel placed a reassured hand on my shoulder. "You're stronger than you think, Breanna. Don't let her rattle you. Focus on what you can control."

I looked up at her, grateful for the support. "Thanks. I needed to hear that."

"Get some rest. Tomorrow's another day, and you'll need your energy."

"Yeah," I managed a genuine smile this time. "I'll try."

She walked away, leaving me alone again. I reclined back in my chair, staring at the ceiling.

Ashley's words replayed in my mind, echoing in the room's silence. "I have big plans," she had said earlier, her eyes locked with mine for a moment. "I think this place could use fresh energy, right?"

I didn't know how to respond then, so I nodded, keeping my opinions to myself. Now, it felt like a challenge.

The newsroom had been my sanctuary, where I'd built my career. I knew its rhythms, its quirks. I knew the people here, and they knew me. Since Ashley's arrival, everything felt different and unsettled.

My phone buzzed on the desk, pulling me from my ideas. It was a text from Aaron. *Outside whenever you're ready.*

I checked the time. It was late. Aaron was waiting for me to wrap up. Grabbing my things, I couldn't ignore the feeling that Ashley's ambition wasn't just professional. The way she hovered around him at the party, testing boundaries, made that clear.

If she made a move. Whatever came next, I'd be ready.

Stepping outside into the cool night, I spotted Aaron by his car. He smiled, and for a moment, the tension eased.

I slipped into the seat, and he looked over with a smile. "Rough day?"

I nodded. "You could say that."

At home, the warmth of the living room wrapped around Aaron and me, and the lamps cast a gentle glow over the space. The day's tension melted as I sank into the couch, pulling a blanket over my lap. I could sense something on his mind, the way his fingers drummed against the armrest, and his eyes searched for the right words.

"Aaron?" I asked, breaking the silence that had settled between us.

He met my gaze, a mixture of determination and uncertainty in his eyes. "Breanna, I've been thinking about something for a while."

"Okay. What is it?"

He took a deep breath, as if gathering his ideas. "I've thought about running for mayor. I would be running against a guy named Martin Brooks. He is a 'yes man' to all the businesses in Centerville."

The words hung in the air, and my heart skipped a beat. I opened my mouth to respond, but nothing came out. My Aaron, who had always been so devoted to his work as the town veterinarian, was about to dive into the political arena. The shift felt enormous, almost surreal.

"You're serious?" I managed to ask, though I could already see the resolve in his eyes.

"Very." His elbows were resting on his knees. "I've been thinking about this for months. I've always wanted to serve, and I love this community. I know I can do some real good here. What we need is strong leadership, someone who truly gets the people. I believe I am that person."

His words stirred something in me, a mix of pride and apprehension. "Aaron, this is huge. It's going to change everything. Our lives, our routines…"

He nodded, his expression softening as he reached across the space between us, taking my hand. "I know, Bre. That's why I wanted to talk to you first. I wouldn't do this without your support."

I squeezed his hand. "It's … a lot to process. You love your work. Being mayor will demand so much more from you. From us."

"I know," he said, his thumb brushing over my knuckles. "I've thought long and hard about this. The town needs someone who cares and who's in it for the right reasons. I want to be that person."

I searched his face, seeing the passion and desire to step up and take on this challenge. His commitment to doing what was admirable was the one thing I loved about him. That didn't make the prospect any less daunting.

"What about us?"

"We'll make it work." His voice was a calm assurance. "We've always faced challenges together, Bre. This won't be any different."

I nodded. The reality of what he was saying sank in. I could see the future unfolding, full of campaign events, late nights, and public scrutiny. It would be a test of our relationship and our resilience. Aaron had always been my anchor. If anyone could handle this, it was him.

"What do you need from me?"

"Your support." His eyes locked onto me. "Your honesty. If you have concerns, I want to hear them."

I nodded again, appreciating the warmth of his hand in mine, grounding me. "You have my support. Always."

He smiled, relief washing over his features, and I felt a slight sense of peace settle in my chest. This would be hard, no doubt about it. But we could do it.

Yet, I couldn't help but think of the challenges ahead, not the campaign, but everything. The people would question his motives. The choices he'd have to make, and where that left us, our life together.

I pulled Aaron closer, resting my head on his shoulder. The future was uncertain, filled with hurdles we couldn't yet see. We would face it, side by side, as we always had. It was late, and tomorrow was another busy day. With a tired sigh, I called it a night before heading to our bedroom.

It was quiet outside. The curtains, drawn tight, filtered the streetlight into a soothing glow. I lay on our bed, the soft rustle of the sheets the only sound breaking the silence. Aaron was downstairs, working on his campaign materials.

I turned to my side, glancing at the space next to me. His pillow was untouched, and his absence reminded us of the new demands on our lives. I reached for my phone, hoping to find a distraction. The screen lit up with his message: *"Almost done here. How's everything on your end?"*

I typed back, *"I'm okay."*

Setting the phone aside, I looked around the room. The soft light from the bedside lamp created gentle shadows on the walls. The room was a refuge, a place to escape from the outside world.

I picked up the framed photo on the nightstand. It was a picture of Aaron and me from our 2nd anniversary trip on a Canadian river cruise. The image was a snapshot of simpler times, a stark contrast to the complexity of our present situation. I traced the rim of the frame with my fingers, trying to hold on to the calm that moment represented.

The implications of Aaron's political aspirations and Ashley's influence created a knot of anxiety in my stomach. It would bring new opportunities and pressures. I'd be standing beside him and trying to manage the changes in our lives.

I turned my back, staring at the ceiling. I had always prided myself on managing personal and professional challenges, but tonight felt different. The balance between supporting him and dealing with her planning was more precarious than ever.

The door creaked, and he appeared, his face tired but determined. "Hey, still awake?" he asked, coming over.

"Yeah," I smiled.

He sat down beside me, the bed shifting.

He reached over, taking my hand. "I know it's overwhelming. We'll get through it together. We've faced challenges before. Such as when you, Holli, Rebeccah, and Samantha went after Chris Fredrick 3 years ago with corruption, bribes, and murder. We can get through this."

I squeezed his hand, grateful for his reassurance. "I'm worried about how it will play out. I need to be ready for whatever comes next."

He nodded, brushing a strand of hair from my face. "You're not alone in this."

The warmth of his touch was comforting. I leaned against him. We lay there in silence. I found solace in the quiet support of his company.

Chapter 3

The council chamber was energetic as the meeting warmed up. The usual mix of whispers and shuffling papers filled the room, punctuated by the ticking of the clock overhead. Rows of committee members exchanged nods and quick words while a few residents watched from the back, waiting for the actual business to begin.

I settled in, a pen hovering over my notebook, trying to focus as the early chatter dragged on. Just another meeting, or so it seemed. Then I heard David Prescott's name slip out, dropping like a stone in still water. My pen pressed down, leaving a deep indentation in my notes.

Mr. Thompson, a usually mild-mannered council member, leaned forward, his voice charged. "We'll review Prescott's involvement in the new development plans tonight." He flipped through his folder. "It's a part of the larger push for Centerville's expansion."

The words came out almost too smoothly, and I didn't buy it for a second. I studied the lines on Thompson's face, tracing the hint of discomfort around his eyes. He hadn't mentioned specifics, but how he said "Prescott's involvement" made the hairs on my neck stand on end.

From across the room, Ms. Carter chimed in, her eyes sharp and focused. "David Prescott's influence over this project could be deeper than it looks. We'll need to keep tabs on it." She slid a look at my way, her expression unreadable.

I scribbled Prescott's name in the margin, underlining it twice. What was he up to? A development project in Centerville? It seemed like another corporate play, but the edges didn't align.

The meeting continued, council members returning to their usual topics, but my thoughts stayed on Prescott. *New developments,* the words pulsed in my mind carrying a vague threat. Centerville was in for more than just a facelift if he held influence here. Prescott's projects never came without a price, and my gut told me this time was no exception. Someone was forcing something on this town, whether townspeople wanted it.

The council adjourned, and people trickled out. But I stayed behind, jotting down every scrap of thought that crossed my mind. Time slipped away unnoticed until the quiet click of the door pulled me back.

Aaron.

He leaned against the doorframe for a beat, watching me, then walked over and slid into the chair beside me. His presence was steady, grounding.

"You planning on moving in here?" he asked, a hint of amusement in his voice.

I blinked, then glanced at my phone. Several *unread messages* from him. Right. I had texted earlier, saying I'd be late, but I got so caught up I forgot to check back.

I exhaled, setting my pen down. "Lost track of time."

He studied me for a second. "You caught something." It wasn't a question, it was a statement, laced with quiet certainty. I wondered how he knew about it.

I hesitated, then met his eyes. "A name kept coming up today." I tapped my pen against the notepad. "David Prescott. They're slipping him into the development plans, and I know there's more to it."

Aaron's brow knit, his jaw setting hard. He leaned on the table, resting his arms on the table, his voice low. "So, what are we dealing with?"

I tapped my notebook, thinking aloud. "The council dropped his name too easily, like they were told to smooth it over. We're looking at more than a development, probably a network of interests Prescott's tied into. And that network? It's growing."

Aaron ran a hand over his face, a muscle twitching in his cheek. "If Prescott's network controls Centerville's expansion, he's stacking the odds for himself and against us. He's been trying to undermine the campaign from the start. This is a strategic move."

I nodded. "He's tying himself to Centerville's growth to make his influence impossible to untangle. And by the time the public realizes, he'll be holding all the cards." I paused, watching Aaron's gaze intensify. "This affects the campaign in ways we can't ignore."

He reached out, tapping the notebook as if weighing our next steps. "We push forward. Dig until we understand every piece of this. Then we make sure the public knows what's happening."

"Agreed." I gathered my things, feeling the weight of what lay ahead but ready. Prescott might have a plan, but we were prepared to disrupt it.

Our living room had never looked like this. Campaign posters covered the walls and spread flyers across the coffee table. Friends and family filled the space, the air buzzing with excitement and nervous anticipation. The hum of hushed conversations and the clinking of glasses created a steady backdrop. In the middle of it all, Aaron stood at the front, a spotlight illuminating his face. He appeared taller and more resolute, as if he had already transformed himself.

I couldn't take my eyes off him. My heart pounded with pride, but something else too, a tightness in my chest, wouldn't ease. I understood what was coming, what this moment meant for both of us.

Aaron cleared his throat, and the room quieted. He met my gaze, a flicker of something unspoken passing between us. He turned to our gathered friends and family.

"Thank you all for being here tonight," he began, his voice steady. "This isn't just an announcement, it's the start of a vision I've held close for years. Centerville needs change, and I believe I can help."

Aaron's gaze swept across the room, catching my eye. A sense of quiet strength radiated from him as he spoke. This wasn't about politics but a genuine commitment to reshaping our town.

"Our community has seen too many projects come and go," he continued, his voice gaining.

Aaron paused, letting his words settle. A flicker of emotion passed over his face, something like pride mixed with determination.

"We need a community center," he said, his voice ringing with conviction. "A place for families to gather, kids to play safely after school, and seniors to feel valued." He took a breath, glancing at the crowd, then continued, "Centerville deserves to be more than just a stop on the map. We're a community, and it's time we feel like one."

People shifted forward in their seats. Aaron was hitting on something everyone felt but rarely voiced.

"And it won't stop there," he said, gripping the edges of the podium. "Our local businesses struggle, and it's time we give them support. If elected, I'll fight to bring grants and training programs to help our small business owners thrive. No more empty storefronts, no more abandoned buildings. Centerville has potential; it just needs the right push."

His words drew murmurs from the back and a few quiet claps from the business owners scattered throughout the crowd.

He glanced down, collecting his thoughts, then looked up, locking eyes with the audience. "We'll also focus on improving our schools. Our teachers deserve resources, and our kids deserve every opportunity we can give them. Education is the heart of a thriving community, and it's high time we prioritize it."

A ripple of approval traveled through the audience, and I saw the hope light up in a few faces. Aaron's plans weren't just ideas; they were promises. And watching him stand there, I knew he meant every word.

As he wrapped up, a soft determination set in his jaw. "Together, we can make Centerville a place that serves everyone, a town people want to raise their kids in, a home we're proud of."

He stepped back, his gaze meeting mine for a split second. A small smile tugged at the corner of his mouth. This wasn't just a campaign to him, it was a commitment; one he was ready to give his all. And watching him stand there, full of conviction, I couldn't have been prouder.

The room went silent, everyone hanging on his words. I spotted the pride in their faces, the way they leaned forward, eager to catch more. Aaron paused, letting the moment settle before he continued.

"I'm announcing my candidacy for mayor of Centerville."

A loud and enthusiastic wave of applause filled the room. People stood, clapping and cheering. The noise swelled, and so did the anxiety twisting in my stomach. I clapped with the others, but my mind raced about what this meant for us.

He smiled, his confidence shining through as he raised a hand to quiet the room. "This will not be easy. We're up against a lot, and I need your support. I'm ready for this challenge and realize we can make a difference."

I glanced around the room, catching the supportive smiles of our friends and family. They believed in him, as I did, but they didn't understand the weight of what he was taking on.

After the clapping stopped, Aaron stepped away and approached me. He looked at me with excitement and determination.

"What do you think?"

"I'm proud of you." I meant every word.

He reached for my hand, squeezing it. "We'll survive this. Together."

I nodded, trying to believe it. "I understand."

The evening continued, and people mingled again. I stayed close to Aaron's side. He was now the center of attention, surrounded by well-wishers offering advice and encouragement. During it all, I kept thinking about the road ahead.

I caught a snippet of conversation between him and Thomas, his manager. He was the strategist, already discussing the next steps and what Aaron needed to do to win. Something in Thomas's tone made me uneasy. His words were too smooth, as if he were playing a game I didn't understand.

Aaron nodded along, absorbing Thomas's advice, but I detected the subtle shift in his expression. He was listening but also wary, which made me even more anxious. I understood he was brilliant, but this world of politics was new. The challenges ahead were about winning votes and keeping our integrity intact.

Aaron's announcement had set something in motion we couldn't stop now. There would be difficulties that would test us in ways we hadn't imagined. I looked at him, still deep in conversation with Thomas, and I recognized one thing for sure: it would be a journey he would not have to face alone.

Thomas's office was a study of organized chaos. Posters competed for space on the walls with strategy charts, while stacks of folders teetered on every flat surface. I sat in the corner, observing the scene, feeling more like an outsider than ever.

Thomas bent over his desk, pointing to something on one chart. He spoke in a measured tone, deliberately choosing each word as he outlined the next steps for Aaron's campaign. "Let's get going. Start with the neighborhoods closest to City Hall, then work our way out. It's about visibility. People need to spot you in the places that matter."

Aaron nodded, his eyes fixed on the chart, absorbing every detail. "After that?"

He straightened, a gleam in his eye I didn't like. "We focus on the media. Get them on your side early. I've got contacts who can help shape the narrative. We'll make sure the story they're telling is what we want."

He spoke with a confidence which bordered on arrogance, and as he continued, I detected the subtle shift in his tone. His suggestions were sharp, but there was something else too—an undertone of self-interest twisted in my gut.

"We need to play this smart. Timing is key. A well-placed comment here, a strategic appearance there… It's all about creating momentum. Trust me, I understand how to build it."

Aaron leaned back in his chair, considering the plan. "What about the debates? How do we handle those?"

He grinned, a quick flash of teeth. "They are a game. You stay calm and focused. You speak to the people, not your opponent. I'll prep you with the talking points, but remember—it's not what you say. It's how you say it. We'll ensure you're the voice of reason in the room."

Thomas's eyes lit up, but not in a way that inspired confidence. I shifted in my seat, the unease tightening in my chest. He was more excited about the game than the goal. It was in the way his gaze lingered on the charts and his hands moved as he spoke. If he were orchestrating something far bigger than Aaron's run for mayor.

Aaron asked another question, and Thomas responded with the same calculated enthusiasm. I tuned out their words, focusing instead on the rhythm of their talk. He was good at this—too good. He understood how to spin a story and guide a conversation to his advantage. It made me wonder: Whose campaign was this?

The session continued with more talk of strategy, timing, and influence. Aaron bought into every word Thomas said, nodding as if the plan were foolproof.

And as I saw them both, my unease grew. Aaron was brilliant, for sure. Yet, politics was unfamiliar territory for both of us.

He stood, extending his hand to Thomas. "Thanks for this. I understand we are more prepared now."

Thomas shook his hand, that same knowing smile on his face. "We've got this. Stick with the plan, and you'll be in City Hall before you know it."

Aaron nodded, turning toward me with a look of excitement and determination. Forcing a smile, I rose to my feet, but the tightness in my chest remained.

We left Thomas's office.

My home office appeared a world apart, lit by the single desk lamp casting long shadows over the scattered papers. The air was thick with the scent of old newsprint and the faint hum of my laptop.

Stacks of newspapers lay open around me, each flagged with sticky notes and highlighted passages. My fingers flashed across the keyboard. I pulled up more articles and scanned for names, dates, and anything that fit into the puzzle I was trying to solve. It started as a small story—a minor city official caught in a questionable deal. The more I dug, the more it flew into something larger.

I leaned back in my chair, eyes narrowing at the latest article on my screen. New jobs, infrastructure, everything the public wanted to take in. The numbers didn't match. They awarded the contracts to companies with hidden connections.

A name kept coming up—David Prescott. A developer with a spotless record who was always in the right place at the right time. There was something about him, something off. They casually mentioned him at the last city council meeting. This wasn't random. Now all the signs were hinting at something big, uncertain and crocked.

My phone buzzed on the desk, breaking my concentration. I glanced at the screen and it was a text from Aaron.

"Are you still working?"

I stared at the message, the tightness in my chest returned. This investigation wasn't going right.

I typed back, "*Yeah, finishing up.*"

I pulled a file from the pile, flipping it open to a list of members. Martin Brook's name jumped out at me, highlighted in yellow. He had connections everywhere, including with Prescott. He'd been so sure when announced his candidacy, almost too confident. Now, with every piece of evidence I uncovered, I couldn't shake the feeling this wasn't about corruption, but power.

I reached for my notebook, jotting down more notes and questions that needed answers. How deep did this go? Who else was involved? How did this intersect with Aaron's cause? The thought made my stomach churn. I understood his trust in Thomas. I couldn't help but worry about where he would lead.

A knock on the door pulled me from my thoughts. Aaron stepped in, his expression softening when he noticed me surrounded by papers. "You're still at it."

"Yeah." My voice was tight. "There's a lot here."

He walked over, glancing at the papers on my desk. "What are you finding?"

"More than I expected," I admitted, leaning back in my chair. "This development deal, it's not clean. There are connections to city council members and people without business involvement."

He frowned, picking up one article I'd printed. "You think this could affect the campaign?"

"I don't know yet. It could touch everything if it's as big as it looks."

Aaron sighed, setting the paper down. "You're good at this. Don't get too wrapped up. We're in this together, remember?"

I nodded. "I know. I … I don't want you blindsided."

He squeezed my shoulder, a gesture of comfort, but I saw the worry in his eyes, too. "Whatever comes, we'll handle it."

He left the room. I returned to my files, the urgency growing. The information started coming together, but what they formed was still unclear. One thing was sure, though: this investigation was not a story. It was something that could change everything for Aaron, for me, and the city. I wasn't positive we were ready for what it would reveal.

CHAPTER 4

I arrived at the studio earlier than usual. The stillness seemed heavy, different from the typical buzz of activity. I couldn't shake the frustration from yesterday. Ashley hadn't shown up for the broadcast. No call, no explanation, nothing. I understood she was reliable, but the silence gnawed at me.

I paced the room, glancing at the clock every few seconds. We had a team, a system. She couldn't vanish without a word.

A creak came from the door. I looked up, ready to demand answers. As she walked in, something stopped me cold. It was her appearance.

She wasn't herself messed up hair. Dark circles and crisp clothes seemed thrown together. This wasn't the person I knew.

I swallowed my surprise and forced myself to stay focused. "Where were you yesterday?"

She hesitated, her hand fidgeting with the strap of her bag. "Something came up."

I didn't have time for vague answers. "We need you here. The entire team depends on it."

She didn't meet my eyes. I noticed her fingers trembling and her breathing shallow. I experienced a pang of guilt, but pushed it aside. This wasn't about her.

"We're a team," I pressed. "Something's going on. You need to tell me."

She peered up then, eyes glassy and distant. She opened her mouth to speak but closed it again, struggling. The silence stretched, my impatience growing. I needed answers, not this drawn-out hesitation.

She spoke in a whisper. "I have breast cancer."

The room tilted. I blinked, processing the words. "What?"

"Stage 3," she continued, like she'd used all her strength to say it. "I'd been processing it for months, but... yesterday was too much. I couldn't do it."

My frustration melted away, replaced by a shock. My mind raced, struggling to reconcile the Ashley I recognized with the reality she'd revealed. How long had she been carrying this alone? The guilt hit me hard, forming a pit in my stomach.

I took a step closer, my voice softer now. "Why didn't you tell me?"

She shrugged, the movement slight, defeated. "I didn't want anyone to know. I thought I could deal with it... until I couldn't."

I reached out, placing a hand on her shoulder. She flinched, then relaxed, the tension easing under my touch. I wanted to say something comforting, something that would make this nightmare easier to bear, but the words stuck in my throat.

"We'll figure this out," I managed, the promise feeling inadequate against the enormity of her situation. "You're not alone in this."

She nodded, a tear slipping down her cheek. I witnessed it fall. I had been ready to reprimand her, to demand explanations. Now, all I wanted was to help her through this.

I stood there with my hand on Ashley's shoulder, the pieces finally clicking into place.

A couple of weeks ago, over coffee, Anna had mentioned someone facing a life-altering diagnosis. She hadn't shared details of confidentiality, she'd said, but the worry in her voice had been real. As a mother, the thought of going through something similar had shaken her.

I'd brushed it off then, assuming it was just another patient. Now, looking into Ashley's tired eyes, I understood. And all this time, she'd been fighting this battle alone—right under my nose. The realization hit hard.

I led her to a secluded corner of the studio, away from the noise of the newsroom. We found a spot near the windows where the morning light softened the sharp edges of the room. I turned to face her, searching her eyes for the secrets she knew, but did not want to tell.

"Tell me more. I want to understand," I said.

She took a deep breath, her shoulders sagging as if the burden of her past was too much to bear. "It's not the first time I've faced something like this," she began, her voice above a whisper.

I frowned, surprised. "What do you mean?"

Her gaze drifted to the window. "I've been fighting battles by myself for a long time. I had leukemia as a kid and spent years in and out of hospitals. My mom didn't make it through her battle with cancer." She paused, her hands trembling as she clasped them together. "It's always been me against this thing. I've always kept it to myself. I didn't want pity."

A lump formed in my throat. I hadn't expected this or imagined the depth of what she'd been carrying alone. "You don't have to do this solo, Ashley. Not this time."

She met my eyes, the exhaustion clear in the dark circles beneath them. "I don't know how to lean on others. I've never had to."

"I understand," I said, nodding. "Things are different now. You have people who care, who want to help."

She let out a shaky breath, her resolve wavering. "I might need more time off. I hate leaving everyone in a bind now."

I perceived the pull between my empathy for her and my responsibility to keep the staff. People would notice her absence during the crucial election. How could I push her when she was already dealing with so much?

"I'll take care of it," I said, the words slipping out before I considered them.

She wrapped her arms around me in a hug, holding on for a moment longer than usual. She turned and walked down the hall, a small but determined figure heading into an uncertain future. I witnessed her go. I vowed to be there for her, no matter what.

The sun dipped in the sky, painting the neighborhood in shades of orange and gold. Aaron and I strolled down the peaceful street, our steps crunching on the gravel. Campaign signs for him dotted the lawns, their bright colors fluttering in the breeze. The warm light made the evening feel nostalgic, a gentle backdrop to our efforts.

We went by a modest house with a mowed lawn. I noticed the hesitant glances of some residents through their windows, their interest fleeting. A few others opened their doors with eager smiles, welcoming Aaron's pitch with genuine curiosity.

Each interaction mattered. His message needed to be interesting, clear, and resonant. I caught myself adjusting the placement of his signs, ensuring they were visible and well-placed.

He approached the next house, his hand reaching for the doorbell. He took a deep breath, as if preparing for another round of questions and small talk. I stood back, watching the scene unfold.

The door creaked open, revealing an older woman with a warm smile. "Good evening," He began. "I'm Aaron Reynolds, and I'm running for mayor. I'd love to take in your thoughts on the upcoming election."

She nodded, her eyes scanning his materials. "I've seen your signs around. What are your plans for the city?"

Aaron met her gaze. "First, I want to focus on revitalizing local businesses by cutting unnecessary red tape so they can grow. Public safety is also a priority. Our first responders need better support, and I'll make sure they get it. We need to concentrate on the infrastructure. We need actual solutions for our roads, not just patchwork fixes."

She considered for a moment. "That all sounds good, but how do you plan to pay for it?"

"I'll push for smarter budgeting," he said. "Cut wasteful spending, prioritize projects that matter, and work with local businesses to create revenue instead of raising taxes."

She nodded slowly. "I appreciate you stopping by, Mr. Reynolds. I'll keep an eye on your campaign."

"Thank you," Aaron said with a smile. "Have a great evening."

We stepped off the porch, I fell into stride beside him as we walked down the narrow walkway. The cool evening air carried the distant hum of crickets.

Near the sidewalk, a familiar figure leaned against a parked truck. It was Thomas.

Aaron gave him a nod. "Evening, Thomas."

"Hey, Breanna, Aaron," Thomas called out, catching his breath. "I want you to see this!"

Aaron gazed up from the conversation with the woman. "What's up?"

He glanced and lowered his voice. "I've been digging into some financial records at the local elementary school. There's some strange stuff going on—transactions that make little sense."

My heart skipped a beat. I had to resist the urge to lean in closer. "What transactions?" I asked, trying to keep my voice unwavering.

He shifted. "It's not one or two. There's a pattern, like someone's funneling money. I think this might connect to a larger problem.

Aaron's eyes narrowed, his mind processing the information. "You think this could affect my campaign?"

Thomas nodded. "It might. It depends on how you address it. Thought you should be aware."

I glanced at Aaron. His expression was thoughtful. The potential for a major scoop or an issue was clear.

His tone measured. "I appreciate you bringing this to us."

Aaron needed to continue his portion of the canvassing, so we both resumed our work. The evening breeze grew colder, and the neighborhood grew quieter. But my mind stayed on the discovery. This could shape Aaron's campaign—or complicate it in ways we hadn't expected.

Aaron and I continued our canvassing, our footsteps muffled by the cool grass and the occasional crunch of gravel. The signs were a reminder of the support Aaron was building.

Aaron stopped and stared at me, his face set with resolve. "We need more information before making any moves."

I nodded. The discovery could change everything, but it also meant stepping into unknown territory. Challenges were only beginning, and the road ahead was uncertain.

The studio was peaceful, the only sound the faint hum of fluorescent lights overhead. Empty chairs stood scattered, papers strewn across the desks, remnants of a long, tense day. I paced the length of my office, each slow step weighted with the decision I had to make. The room appeared heavy, the silence pressing in on me.

I paused before my desk, eyes landing on a framed photo. The picture showed our staff smiling and full of life; a reminder of the camaraderie we'd built. I picked it up, tracing a finger over the glass. This wasn't about me. It was about the team, the people who relied on me and each other.

With a sigh, I set the photo back down and reached for my phone. My fingers trembled as I searched my contacts until I found Rachel's number. I pressed the call button and listened to the dial tone, my heart pounding.

"Rachel," I said when she answered. "I need your advice."

"What's going on?" Her voice was calm, reassured, and always cut through the chaos.

"It's Ashley," I said, sinking into my chair. "She asked for time off. It's bad. She's struggling, and I don't know what to do."

She was silent, and I could almost perceive her thinking, weighing her response. "How is it?"

"She's falling apart," I admitted, acknowledging the words. "I want to help her, but I don't know how without putting the team under more stress."

"Breanna, support her. She's asking for time. She needs it. The group will understand. You can't be afraid to lean on them."

I glanced around the empty studio, imagining how it would function without Ashley. "I can manage the extra work, but I'm worried about the long-term impact. The show can't afford to lose momentum."

"You need to plan," Rachel said. "Organize temporary coverage and use resources. Employee support and counseling—whatever she needs, ensure she gets it. Take care of yourself, too. This won't be easy, but you don't have to do it by yourself."

A small smile tugged at the corners of my lips. She always had a way of making things seem manageable, even when they felt overwhelming. "Thanks. I appreciate it."

"Anytime, Breanna. Remember, you're not a co-anchor. You're a leader, and your team trusts you."

The line went dead, and I set the phone down. I had decided. Now, I had to follow through.

I prepared for the next morning's broadcast, and a soft knock on the door interrupted me, pulling me from my thoughts. Ashley stood in the doorway, her shoulders hunched, her eyes downcast. She held a formal leave request form in her hands, her grip tight as if it were the only thing keeping her grounded.

Sitting down on a chair next to me, "I need some time off," she said, her voice clear. "I wouldn't ask if I didn't need it."

I nodded, taking the form from her. I could see the strain on her face, the exhaustion that no amount of makeup could hide. She was breaking, and I knew I couldn't let her go through this alone.

"Take the time you need," I said. "We'll manage here, and no one needs to learn what's going on until you're ready. I've got your back, Ashley."

She peered up at me, her eyes filled with gratitude and something else. Fear, maybe. Fear of being judged, fear of losing her place. "Thank you, Breanna. I don't realize how to thank you."

"You don't have to," I said, squeezing her shoulder. "Focus on getting better. We'll be here when you're ready to come back."

She nodded, a hint of relief softening her expression. She turned to leave, but paused at the door. "I'll be back as soon as I can. I promise."

"I know you will," I said, watching her walk away, the door closing behind her.

I sat down at my desk, pulled out a notepad, and jotted down the tasks that would need coverage. There were schedules to rearrange, responsibilities to shift, and a staff to keep motivated.

I worked, and the reality of the situation settled in. It wasn't about covering for Ashley. Rachel's words echoed in my mind. It was about maintaining the trust of our audience, making sure that our team didn't crumble under pressure.

I realized I would need help from my colleagues to finish the work. Even as I made my plans, a nagging feeling remained. Real challenges weren't here yet, but ahead.

Chapter 5

As I entered the charity event, the room was so alive with chatter and laughter. Tension was on edge, much like when I'd first learned David Prescott's name. His introduction registered in the crowd, but it hit me like a cold draft, and I watched him more than listened to the speeches. Something about him tugged at the part of me that realized this was not another charity gala.

He moved through the crowd with effortless charm, shaking hands, flashing that perfect smile. Dark hair, sharp suit, piercing blue eyes, a picture of success. Too polished. Too smooth.

"Prescott's done well for himself," a voice nearby said, and I witnessed two women chatting near the bar. "Having his hand in everything."

I turned, eyes narrowing, as David approached a small circle of local politicians. His smile stayed plastered in place, but I spotted the way his gaze shifted, calculating.

"You realize," he said, his voice loud enough to carry, "you can get anything done in this town if you know the right people."

The comment was casual, but it landed on me. My reporter's instincts flared. He had said it like a joke, but the way his lips curled after made me think it was not.

Someone next to him chuckled. "Is that how you've been so successful?"

He tilted his head, raising an eyebrow. "Let's say there are ways through the usual red tape." He sipped his drink, his eyes gleaming with a hint of something I couldn't quite name.

I detected the knot tightening in my stomach. I wasn't sure I wanted to understand, but couldn't ignore it.

I peeked around the room, watching how people leaned in when he talked and how no one questioned him. He had power here. I didn't have the complete picture, but I could detect its edges pressing in.

The night passed in a blur of faces and conversations, yet my attention stayed locked on David Prescott. I noticed him as he worked through the crowd, his smile never faltering.

He mingled among the crowd, his laughter ringing out, drawing even more people in. Every gesture and word designed to reinforce his image.

As the evening progressed, I caught more snippets of conversation. David's name appeared, often accompanied by vague remarks about his influence and success.

I tried to piece together his interactions, noting the subtle way he shifted topics or deflected questions. He was careful, almost too thorough. His charisma seemed like a smokescreen.

As the event ended, I sensed a gnawing certainty that Prescott was not what he seemed. His charm was too smooth, his influence too pervasive. I was determined to peel back the layers and discover what he was concealing.

This wasn't idle curiosity. He was hiding something significant, and I was going to uncover it.

I got home and sank into my desk chair, the dim light from the lamp casting long shadows across the scattered documents. They carried the burden of the entire investigation. I stared at the papers and bids, trying to make sense of the mess before me. David Prescott's name wasn't on them, but something about their patterns seemed off.

The files detailed city development agreements with favorable terms and signatures that didn't agree. Irregularities were clear, but the connection to Prescott wasn't clear.

The information suggested something significant, but it was like chasing shadows without concrete links to Prescott himself.

Determined, I reached out to Samantha. Samantha was a long-time college friend and had a mystery about her. As a computer whiz, her talent for uncovering hidden details was apparent to me. She is a valuable resource to have, but I did not call on her computer services often. She was a great friend and had been the matron of honor at my wedding. After a few minutes, I caught her familiar voice on the other end of the line.

"Hey, it's Breanna," I said. "I'm hitting a wall with this investigation. I need your help."

"What's up?" her tone was curious and attentive.

"I'm looking at these contracts and financial statements. There are irregularities, suspicious signatures, odd payments, but nothing linking him to the wrongdoing. I want some concrete ties to the developer. His name is David Prescott."

Samantha was silent for a moment. "Alright, let me dig into it. I'll investigate what I can find. I'll call you back soon."

I ended the call, sensing a sliver of hope. With Samantha's help, I discovered that missing link. The frustration still settled in my chest, and the connections remained elusive. I understood this was the beginning, and I had to keep pushing. Each step, no matter how small, was crucial in unraveling the truth.

I continued to sift through the papers, and Aaron walked in. He looked over at me, concern etched on his face.

"Working on that Prescott case?" he asked, noticing the stack of records before me.

"Yeah," I replied, rubbing my eyes. "I've got agreements and financials with many irregularities, but nothing that ties Prescott to anything. I'm waiting for Samantha to help find a concrete link."

Aaron nodded, walking over to stand behind my chair. "You're making good progress. It can take a while to understand the complete picture."

"I hope so," I said. "I'll keep you posted on what I find."

Aaron's reassured hand lingered on my shoulder before he stepped back. "Let me know if you need resources, a sounding board. I'm here to help."

I saw him leave the room, his footsteps fading down the hallway. Alone, I stood still for a moment, absorbing his offer. I began pacing the small space of my office, each step echoing my growing concern. Prescott wasn't a businessman; he didn't conduct business transactions. The repercussions of exposing him felt daunting and heavy.

I stopped at the window, looking out at the tranquil streets below. How should I handle this information? Going public could bring down more than Prescott. His contributions reached into schools, parks, and small businesses. Hiding this felt like letting him get away with it.

I waited for Samantha's call. Without her insights, I didn't have all the information yet. The pressure of the decision weighed on me. I needed to balance the truth against its potential fallout. If release this, I risked everything. If I didn't, I might let corruption continue unchecked.

I sat by the window, watching the empty street below as my thoughts raced. Every second stretched longer than the last. I kept replaying the conversation with Samantha, hoping she'd find something solid, something I could use.

The soft ring of my phone shattered the silence. I grabbed it, my heartbeat quickening.

"Samantha?"

"It's me," she said, her voice steady. "I've dug up some things."

I leaned forward, gripping the edge of my desk. "What did you find?"

"There's a connection, Breanna," she said, the weight of her words sinking in. "I traced some of those questionable payments. They're funneled through a series of businesses, all tied to a man named Robert Greene. He's Prescott's go-to guy for shady deals. Nothing shows Prescott's name, but Greene supports almost every development contract you've been looking into."

"Robert Greene," I repeated, jotting the name down. "So, he's using him to stay clean, letting him handle the dirty work."

"Exactly," Samantha said. "It's not enough to convict him, but it's a start. It paints a picture of how Prescott operates without leaving a trail."

I breathed, the frustration loosening its grip, but only. "It's something, but it's still not enough."

"I know," she said. "It's the crack in the investigation you needed. Follow this, and more will come up."

I nodded to myself, grateful, but still weighed down. "Thanks. I couldn't have gotten this far without you."

"Keep digging, Breanna," she urged. "I'll stay on it too. We'll get there."

I hung up, the name Robert Greene echoing in my head. It was a step, but not the one that would bring Prescott down. I pushed back from my desk, pacing again, my thoughts swirling. He was too careful, too brilliant. He was his cover, and I had to expose that connection.

Aaron walked back into the room; his face etched with calm concern. "You, okay?"

I nodded, though the uncertainty still clung to me. "Samantha found something. Prescott's been using a guy named Robert Greene to cover his tracks. It's a link, but not enough."

"What's your next move?"

I stared at the floor for a moment, then back at him. "I must follow this lead. Dig deeper into Greene and see if there's a way to connect him to Prescott. I can do that. I'll have the proof I need."

He watched me, then nodded. "You'll get there. Take your time. You don't have to do this alone."

I reached for his hand, grateful for the reassurance he always offered. "I won't. I take this public... it could destroy everything Prescott's built. His reputation, his business, everything."

Aaron's grip tightened around mine. "He's guilty."

I met his glance. "You're right. I'll be ready."

I peeked out the window; the street outside was still and quiet. The town seemed peaceful, but I knew it wasn't. Not with Prescott pulling strings.

I rubbed my temples. "It's not that simple."

"I know."

I stood up, pacing the room. "If I make this public. It'll blow up everything. Prescott's tied into lots. Schools, parks, even some businesses that keep this town alive."

Aaron crossed his arms. "So, what's the alternative? Let him keep doing what he's doing?"

I stopped facing him. "No, but what if I'm wrong? What if this isn't enough, and I destroy everything for nothing?"

He sighed, stepping closer. "You're not wrong. You don't have the last piece yet."

I shook my head, the frustration boiling over. "It's not about being right. It's about what happens after. People trust him. They rely on him."

His hand landed on my shoulder, grounding me for a second. "How many people get hurt because they don't know the truth?"

I didn't have an answer to that. I looked at the files again. He was right, but it didn't make the choice any easier.

"I need more time," I said.

He squeezed my shoulder and then let go. "You'll sort it out. Just remember, time isn't endless."

He left the room, his footsteps fading down the hallway, leaving me alone with my thoughts. I stared at the mess of documents, knowing that time wasn't on my side. I needed to act.

Morning came, and I found myself tucked in a corner of the studio, staring at the blank screen of my laptop. The hum of the early routine buzzed around me, but my mind was elsewhere. I couldn't shake the events of the night before. Samantha had come through, like she always did, piecing together the missing links I couldn't find on my own.

The files she uncovered weren't suspicious—they were damning. Prescott's fingerprints were all over them, hidden behind layers of false names and backdoor deals. It wasn't speculation anymore. I had the proof that could tear down his entire empire.

Ashley walked into the studio, her movements slow and deliberate. She paused when she saw me; her stare settling in my tense posture. I looked up from the papers spread across my desk, my heart racing at the sight of her.

Her face was pale, framed by hair that looked more frazzled than usual. She forced a small smile, but it didn't reach her eyes.

"Good morning," I greeted Ashley, trying to muster a smile despite the exhaustion etched into my face. "How did your night go?"

She moved to the chair across from me and sat down, her eyes searching mine with a hint of concern. "Not too bad. What about yours?"

I sighed, rubbing my eyes to chase away the weariness. "It was rough. I am working on a story with David Prescott. He has been more frustrated than I expected. He came across as arrogant. He bragged about getting things done with minimal red tape. It didn't sit right with me."

Ashley's brows furrowed. "What did you find out?"

I leaned forward, resting my elbows on the desk. "I went home and dug into Prescott's background, but it was like trying to catch smoke with my bare hands. There's very little concrete information out there about him. He had a knack for staying out of the limelight, keeping everything secret."

She fixed her stare on me, her concern deepening. "That sounds frustrating. What's the next step?"

I glimpsed at the scattered papers strewn across my desk. "I'm still trying to piece together the puzzle. There's something off about how he operates, but I desire more. It's a waiting game for now, hoping for a break."

"I need to talk to you about Prescott."

I set the files aside and gestured for her to sit. She settled into the chair across from me, hands trembling as she placed the folder on the desk. Her stare never left mine, searching for something—understanding, maybe, or a willing ear.

"There's something else," she said, her voice gaining strength. "I know about Prescott. More than anyone else does."

My eyes narrowed. "What do you know?"

"Actually," Ashley began, "I have to confess something."

I raised an eyebrow, curious. "Go ahead."

Ashley hesitated, her fingers fiddling with the edge of her chair. "I came across some information about the corruption while working on a story for the network. I couldn't pursue it because of my illness."

Ashley's voice wavered as she continued, her stare fixed on the floor. "The story I was working on involved the city's development projects. I came across some documents and internal memos that pointed to Prescott's manipulation of the bidding process. He pressured city officials to award deals to specific firms, which then subcontracted work to lesser-known companies."

She looked up, her eyes filled with regret and determination. "I couldn't follow up because my illness took over, and I had to step back. The evidence suggested that Prescott was orchestrating a scheme to profit from overblown project costs and kickbacks."

Her words illuminated the corruption I had been struggling to understand. The connections she revealed complemented the irregularities I had discovered, but added a crucial detail. Prescott's influence wasn't behind-the-scenes maneuvering; it was about exploiting the system for personal gain, leaving a trail of financial misconduct.

I had only seen Ashley as a diligent journalist, but now a different picture has emerged. She was a colleague; she had been fighting her battles, uncovering the truth despite struggles.

"Wow," I said, trying to process this extra layer of her story. "I did not know."

Ashley's eyes met mine, a mixture of regret and resolve. "It wasn't easy. I wanted to follow through, but my health took precedence. I guess that's why I admire what you're doing. You're picking up where I left off."

Her confession shifted into something in me. I saw her not as a professional, but as someone who had endured and persevered. Her vulnerability made her strength more apparent.

"I did not know," I repeated, my voice steady. "I'm sorry you had to deal with all that. There's anything I can do to help?"

Ashley raised her hand, cutting me off. "It's okay. Knowing someone's continuing the work I started is enough for me."

Her gesture was both humbling and inspiring. I admired her courage, and it deepened my sense of connection. We were striving for the same goal, each in our way.

"Thank you," I said, feeling a new respect for her. "Let's keep pushing forward."

She smiled, a flicker of relief passing across her face. "We can make a difference."

She left the room. I sat back, the day's revelations settling around me. The corruption was bigger than I'd imagined, and so were the people fighting it. With my mind still wrestling with the scandal, I knew I needed advice. Rachel was the one I trusted to offer a clear perspective. I dialed her number and waited as the phone rang.

"Hello?" Rachel's voice was warm and welcoming.

"It's Breanna," I said. "I need to talk. Can we meet?"

"Of course. Where should we go?"

We agreed to meet at a serene café downtown. I arrived to find her already seated with a steaming cup of coffee. Her expression shifted from pleasant to concerned as she saw me.

"Hey. What's going on?" she asked, her eyes searching mine for answers.

I sat and laid out the records I had been poring over. "I've hit a crossroads with the investigation. I've uncovered significant evidence, but I'm torn about how to proceed."

She scanned the papers, her brow furrowing. "What's making you hesitate?"

I felt the last few days' fatigue. "It's not Prescott. If I expose him, it could shake up the entire town. This mess involves Aaron's campaign. I'm worried about the fallout for him."

She nodded, sipping her coffee. "You're right to be cautious. Exposing Prescott might not affect him. It could affect his influence with Brooks if he wins."

The idea hit me hard. Aaron's campaign was important not for him but for the town's future. I ran a hand through my hair. "I need to balance doing what's right with the potential damage. How do I make this decision?"

Rachel's glance softened as she leaned in. "It would help if you weighed the immediate impact against the long-term effects. Consider whether the town needs to know outweighs the risk to Aaron. Sometimes, holding back is a way to protect the greater good."

Her words echoed in my mind. The dilemma between journalistic integrity and personal.

Rachel reached out, placing a hand on my arm. "Whatever you decide, make sure it's something you can live with. You're the only one who can balance this scale."

Her support was a slight comfort, but I knew the choice was mine alone. With a deep breath, I packed up the documents and headed out of the café, my thoughts swirling. The path ahead was uncertain, and I had to find the right balance between revealing the truth and protecting those I cared about.

Chapter 6

Aaron's campaign was in full swing, and energy in his campaign was proof of that. Bright, bold yard signs sprout up on every corner, their colors vivid against the backdrop of the neighborhood. The office hums with activity—volunteers pinning flyers, making calls, planning events. Aaron kept pushing forward, relentless. And the toll of all the work was visible from his tired face-lines.

"Honey, you seem exhausted," I said, trying to offer a sympathetic smile.

"I am, but we had to keep pushing. Brooks was now surging in the polls. I could fight it off, but it's taking everything I have. I don't realize how much more I can give."

"I am here for you," I reassured him, my voice steady despite the turmoil.

"Thanks," looking at me with tired eyes. "I sensed like we were drifting apart."

"I understand. This story on Prescott had consumed all my time. I want to support you, but I need to finish this first."

Aaron had sunk into a chair, his shoulders slumping under his fatigue. "I'm sorry. This whole thing was wearing me down. I needed to focus on what I could control."

I had moved closer, sitting beside him. Our fingers brushed as I took his hand, squeezing it. "We'll manage through this. We've faced difficult times before. This is another challenge."

Aaron's grip on my hand had tightened, and I had spotted some of the tension ease from his posture. "I didn't know what I'd do without you."

Despite the reassurance in that quiet moment, the reality of the campaign's demands didn't shift. Each day still brought new challenges and heightened stress. We both understood that our brief respite wouldn't alter the relentless pace of the campaign. Our shared resolve became a source of strength, reinforcing our commitment to navigate the storm together.

Aaron focused on tightening his strategy. He held more town hall meetings, engaged more with local issues, and ramped up his outreach efforts. He found a new well of determination. He used the frustration as fuel, channeling it into more effective tactics.

I continued working on the Prescott story, knowing it was critical for my career and understanding the broader implications. Recent evidence I uncovered strengthened the corruption narrative, adding more urgency to Aaron's campaign.

We navigated the intense schedule and made slight adjustments to ensure we didn't lose sight of each other. This moment became our sanctuary amidst the chaos, allowing us to reconnect and support.

Aaron and I had dinner in our living room, trying to make the most of our time together. He stared at me with a mixture of gratitude and concern.

"I don't understand how you manage it all," he said, reaching across the table to hold my hand. "You've been my rock through this whole thing."

I smiled, sensing a calm before the storm. "We're in this together," I replied. "We'll face whatever comes our way. The campaign, the story- everything. We've always found a way through."

Aaron's faint but genuine grin returned, and he nodded. The tension in his shoulders eased a little more, and we returned to our separate tasks.

After his smile reassured me, we moved back to our tasks. And so, the movement pressed on with the Prescott story in need of my focus. We visited the election office, ready to support the grassroots and gauge the latest developments.

We settled into our routine, and Ashley's arrival at our home brought a fresh wave of hope. Her determination reinvigorated the office, seamlessly merging with our efforts. It was an unexpected relief. She refused to let the strain of her illness hold her back. Her face was pale, and her movements were slow, but her strength shone through.

She went over and sat where we had gathered at our dining room table. She hunched over a stack of files, her fingers flying across a notepad. Her focus was intense, her hand moving with a speed that didn't fit the situation. After all the whispers I'd heard, seeing her here felt off.

Someone had warned me about this behavior. My instinct to dig deeper flared. If the rumors were true, she was hiding something—or at least operating under her agenda. I needed to monitor her, no question.

She glanced up, her eyes fierce despite her exhaustion. "I'm not letting this illness keep me from helping. Aaron needs every advantage he can get."

Her resolve was inspiring. Ashley's deep knowledge of media strategy had already made a difference. We worked side by side. Her input shaped Aaron's approach to the campaign. She suggested targeting specific demographics and refining messaging based on recent voter feedback.

During an intense session, Ashley slid a folder across the table. "You need to view this," she said, her voice above a whisper. Inside were papers revealing Prescott's extensive connections and financial dealings, painting a clearer picture of the corruption scandal.

"This is incredible," I said, scanning the details. "How did you dig this up?"

She rubbed her tired eyes but managed a weary smile. "I had a hunch there was more. Prescott's ties run deep, and his connections reach far beyond what we thought."

The additional evidence was a fundamental change. The reports detailed payments linked to David and other city officials, which could shift the narrative.

Aaron, seeing the fresh determination in Ashley's eyes, managed a grin. "I can't thank you enough. Your insights are invaluable."

Ashley gave a slight nod, her exhaustion forgotten. "Keep pushing forward. We need to leverage this."

Ashley's sacrifice strengthened our resolve. Her dedication was unwavering. Her help extended beyond the Prescott story. She was crucial in devising strategies for Aaron's media appearances and managing crisis communications.

Aaron and I worked late into the night, strategizing and refining our approach. Bolstered by Ashley's insights, Aaron stepped up his public appearances with purpose. The campaign's energy shifted.

I glanced around the office. He seemed reinvigorated. Ashley, though weary, wore a look of quiet satisfaction. Her efforts have not only given us a more straightforward path.

Aaron turned to us. "We've got a solid plan now."

We parted ways for a few hours of sleep, knowing that the road ahead was still fraught with challenges. We were not surviving the chaos, but using it to our advantage.

Aaron was tired but focused, sat at the head of the table. The walls, adorned with posters and strategy charts, closed in on us, a reminder of the stakes.

I lay out the details from the previous night. "We refined our media plan," I said, spreading the notes and documents. "We need to approach the upcoming interviews with these new angles. We're also preparing a crisis response plan."

Thomas walked in. An expression replaced his usual easygoing demeanor. "I've got something you need to see."

Aaron's attention shifted. "What's up?"

Thomas pulled out a folder and laid it on the table. "I've been digging into Martin Brooks. I found some information showing questionable financial dealings and connections to shady figures."

The room fell silent. Thomas' revelation was intense. I studied his face. He peered, both intrigued and apprehensive.

Aaron flipped through the folder, his brows furrowing. "This could be a significant change. But... using this might backfire. It's risky."

I met his gaze, experiencing the pressure of the moment. "This information could sway the election, but we must handle it. We don't want to be seen as playing dirty. It might turn the voters against us."

Aaron glanced at Thomas. "How sure are you about this?"

Thomas's eyes met Aaron's with unwavering confidence. "The documents are solid. We need to use them, but we need to be strategic. Timing and presentation matter."

Aaron rubbed his temples, and his frustration was clear. "I need to think this through. We might use this information, but we risk losing public trust."

I placed a reassured hand on his arm. "We'll use this crossing no lines."

He took a deep breath, weighing the options. "Alright. Draft a plan, and be prepared for any backlash."

Thomas nodded, satisfied with the plan. "I'll help draft the strategy."

The meeting wrapped up, the team dispersed, and we lost in our thoughts. Thomas's information might be pivotal, but we had to navigate this minefield. The tension in the room lingered as we prepared for the next steps, knowing that every decision would shape the campaign's outcome.

I sat at my desk, and the information began falling into place. Ashley's documents and Samantha's intel converged into a clearer picture. The connections between Prescott, Brooks, and the broader corruption scandal were emerging.

I opened the files, and the hum of the office was a constant backdrop to my focused thoughts. "This transaction here," I said to Ashley, pointing at one of Prescott's finances, "matches a payment Brooks's campaign received."

She leaned closer, her expression intent. "That's a significant connection. It may tie Prescott to Brooks."

I nodded. "If Brooks is involved with him, it might explain his recent poll surge. They might be working together."

With the connections becoming more apparent, I realized the story needed to be broadcast. "We'd like to get this on the evening news," I said. "This can be the turning point in the effort."

Ashley agreed, her face a mix of exhaustion and determination. "We'll need to make sure that the story is airtight."

This information could shift the election in Aaron's favor, but convincing him to use it will be challenging. Aaron was determined to win without appearing to run a smear campaign. It would be a delicate balance that required me to respect his wishes while ensuring the truth came out.

Chapter 7

The park project was Aaron's way of showing the public that actual change was possible. It wasn't a clean-up but about rebuilding a forgotten space, symbolizing what his campaign stood for—renewal, growth, and community. The town neglected this park for years, making it an eyesore that reflected the town's struggles. We could turn it around, sending out the message that Aaron wasn't talking about transformation. He was living it.

That's why the task was essential to his campaign. It wasn't a photo op, but tangible proof we could improve things. We needed people to witness it. I arranged for a live shot during the news.

As the crew finished setting up, I stood in front of the camera, microphone in hand. Behind me, aides were already working, pulling weeds, raking leaves, and sweeping up debris. The air was cool, with a light breeze carrying a scent of cut grass.

"Alright, Breanna, you're on in three," the cameraman said.

I took a breath, focusing on the recreational area. "Good morning, this is Breanna Roberts," I said into the camera. "We're here at the corner of Fairview and Oak. A group of workers is hard at work revitalizing what was once a forgotten piece of our neighborhood. This park initiative, spearheaded by mayoral candidate Aaron Roberts, aims to transform this neglected space into something the entire town can take pride in."

I stepped aside to let the camera pan over the helpers, then continued. "This isn't about cleaning up. It's about taking back our neighborhood, one small piece at a time." With the last words spoken, I gave a subtle nod to the crew. The camera light clicked off. I reached for the mic, signaling the end of the shot.

"Thanks, everyone," I said, hitting send on the shot to the studio.

I returned the microphone to the cameraman and scanned the park. I noticed a young woman hunched over by the playground, picking up trash with a determined focus. Something about her energy that caught my attention.

I approached her, noticing her quick, deliberate movements, which suggested she was fighting more than litter. "You're really into this," I said, stepping closer.

She glanced up, a slight smile breaking through her concentration. "It's gotta finish, right? No one else is going to do it."

I nodded, admired her grit. "I'm Breanna," I said, extending a hand.

"Olivia," she replied, shaking it. Her grip was stronger than I expected, but it matched the fire I noticed in her eyes.

"So, what brought you out here?" I asked curiously.

"My dad used to bring me here when I was a kid." She glanced at the run-down playground. "It was our spot. After he lost his job, we stopped coming. It seemed like the park gave up on us as the town did. I guess I'm here to prove it doesn't have to stay that way."

Her words hit me. I might detect the personal battle behind them, a struggle beyond cleaning up a park. "We're trying to do the same thing," I said, looking around at the workers. "Aaron's hoping this undertaking will show the community transformation is possible."

Olivia nodded, her face softening. "It's a good thing. People need to observe."

She bent back down, picking up a piece of trash and tossing it into the bag slung over her shoulder. I viewed her, sensing she was more than another volunteer. She was part of this place's heartbeat, reflecting the people Aaron advocated for.

"We're glad to have you here," I said, feeling connected to her, knowing, like this playground, she wasn't giving up. Neither were we.

The adventure was gaining momentum, but the genuine spark came when Olivia stepped in. She had a natural fire in her that was hard to ignore.

"Breanna, we can make this project happen," she said, her eyes broad with determination as we walked through the overgrown grass of the park. "The people here need something to believe in."

I studied her for a moment. Her optimism was infectious, but there was a depth behind it. Her shoulders tensed, and her smile faltered when she thought no one was looking. I might tell she was carrying more than she let on.

"Olivia, you've been pushing this so hard," I said, keeping my tone steady. "I understand there's something else."

She glanced at the ground, her hands clenching around the edges of the clipboard she carried. "It's not the playground," she admitted. "My dad lost his job last month. Mom's been sick for a while now... It's getting harder to keep things together."

My chest tightened at her words. I remembered that emotion—being young and carrying more than anyone should. It reminded me of when I first started—battling to make a difference while feeling like everything was falling apart.

"I understand it," I said, keeping my voice firm. "It's a lot to handle."

She smiled, but it didn't quite reach her eyes. "I don't want to let anyone down. This project ... It's about giving people hope. My dad... he's always talking about how the town used to be, how we had something to be proud of."

We moved through the recreation area, discussing plans for clean-up days and how to get more helpers involved. I observed how Olivia's face lit up with every new idea. She was relentless, despite the burden she carried. Something drove her when things got difficult.

"You know," I said after a moment, "you remind me of myself when I was younger."

She peered at me, surprised. "Really?"

I nodded. "Same determination, fire, and drive to affect the world."

She laughed, a sound releasing some of her tension. "Well, let's hope I can make half the difference you've made."

I realized she wasn't helping us with the park. She showed us what struggling meant when the odds seemed stacked against you. She was a force, and I could see how her struggle mirrored the fight Aaron and I were in. The challenges weren't personal—they were about the heart of this town.

Olivia kneeled by a patch of stubborn weeds, pulling them free from the earth with steady hands. Her face flushed from the sun but didn't slow down. The venture had become her mission, and she treated every task with the same determination, no matter how small.

"You don't stop, do you?" I asked, leaning against the shovel I'd used to clear debris.

Olivia glanced up, wiping her brow with the back of her hand. "I can't afford it. If I do, everything might fall apart."

There was something in her voice. I didn't press her on it, though. I understood that sentiment when all was on the brink of collapsing. You keep moving, hoping momentum will hold the pieces together.

"Things become difficult sometimes," I said, tossing the shovel aside.

Olivia stood, dusting off her hands, and her eyes caught mine. "You've done this before, haven't you?"

I nodded. "More times than I'd like to admit."

She smiled, but it didn't last. "My dad says the same thing. He keeps telling me the town used to be different—better. Now, it seems like no one cares anymore."

"People care. They're buried under too much. Sometimes it takes something like this to remind them."

She sighed, the family's struggles to show on her face. "The park is something I can control. I can make it better. Everything else appears so out of reach."

I nodded, understanding. "What you're doing here matters."

Olivia's drive wasn't her burden. I witnessed it in Aaron and noticed it myself. She was pushing through her battles like we were. Her family's struggles differed from ours.

I stepped closer. "It's real. It's what he and I are going through."

Olivia blinked, surprised. "You mean, with the campaign? I thought you both had it under control."

I let out a short laugh. "We're trying. There's so much we can't control. It looks like everything's hanging by a thread."

She nodded, her expression softening. "That sounds familiar."

I kneeled next to her, pulling at the roots of a thick weed. "The trick is to keep going when it seems impossible."

Olivia's eyes flickered with understanding. "You think we can win?"

"I think we don't have a choice," I said, meeting her gaze. "We must push. If we don't, people like Martin Brooks win."

The wind shifted, blowing through the park. I realized the battles ahead weren't for the campaign or the playground.

"We're not giving up," I said, standing and offering her a hand. "Not in this town."

She took my hand, her grip firm. "Neither am I."

The task had finally started gaining traction. Volunteers showed up daily, and the park was transforming. Aaron's movement was riding on this momentum. We needed this win—something tangible for the town to believe in.

It began with small things. Permits that were supposed to be routine took weeks instead of days. Funds promised were now "under review" by committees and didn't exist until. I couldn't shake the impression someone was pulling strings behind the scenes.

One morning, as I sat in the office going through paperwork, Aaron walked in, his face tight. He tossed a letter onto my desk. "This is the third delay this week."

I picked it up and scanned its contents. There was another notice about the park's permit being delayed due to "unforeseen administrative issues." I noticed a knot form in my stomach. "This isn't normal."

Aaron leaned against the desk, crossing his arms. "No, it's not. They're doing this on purpose."

"Prescott's people?" I asked, knowing the answer.

He nodded. "Who else? His allies are all over these community boards. They'll do whatever it takes to slow us down."

I set the letter down, frustration bubbling beneath the surface. "They're using bureaucracy as a weapon. If they can't stop us outright, they'll drown us in red tape."

Aaron's gaze hardened. "I can fight it, but it'll take time. Time is something we don't have."

We both recognized it. The election was fast approaching, and every delay chipped away at the momentum we'd built. We couldn't push back now, or else the project would stall. It would look like we were incompetent and couldn't deliver on our promises.

Olivia came to the park. She had been a constant presence, working harder than most volunteers despite everything she dealt with. Today, she appeared frustrated, her usual energy replaced by quiet anger.

"They're spreading rumors," she said, not bothering with pleasantries. She dropped a stack of flyers onto the bench beside me. "People are saying the funding for this initiative isn't legitimate. They're questioning where the money's coming from."

I picked up the flyer. The message contained subtle but pointed phrases like "transparency" and "accountability," all designed to cast doubt without outright accusations.

I wonder who did this? I asked, "Who's behind this?"

Olivia shrugged. "Probably the same people who've been delaying the permits. They don't want this project to succeed."

I sensed a chill run down my spine. "They're trying to discredit the whole initiative."

We weren't dealing with bureaucratic delays or rumors anymore. This was a deliberate power-play designed to tear down everything we'd worked for. Prescott's reach went further than I'd thought.

"They're stalling to protect him," I muttered, thinking out loud. "If this project succeeds, it'll show the town we don't need him or his businesses to rebuild."

Aaron joined us, his expression serious as he looked at the flyer. "We can't let this happen."

They played a quiet game, using whispers and delays to sap our strength. To beat them, we needed to be equally calculated.

"We push back," I said, a plan forming. "We call out the delays, the rumors. We make it public. Let the town witness what's happening here."

Aaron stared at me, considering it. "That could work. We need concrete evidence to show how Prescott's people are involved."

I nodded. "I'll start digging. There's more to this than we're seeing."

Olivia's eyes flickered with determination. "Whatever you need, I'm in."

The local diner buzzed with conversation. Chelsea and I settled into a booth by the window. I wrapped my hands around the warm cup, seeking comfort from the hot tea. The steam rose and blurred my vision, a brief respite from outside chaos.

She took a sip from her cup, her eyes fixed on me with concern. "So, what's been going on?" she asked, her voice calm.

I stared into my coffee, watching the ripples dance on the surface. "The park project, it's a mess. What started as a simple idea to engage the community has become a nightmare."

She asked, voicing her curiosity, "How so?"

I sighed, trying to find the right words. "They've delayed the permits." Funding is in question. It's like someone's ready to sabotage it, and on top of Aaron's campaign is faltering. "The timing couldn't be worse."

She reached across the table, placing a comforting hand over mine. "You've got a lot on your plate. This investigation, supporting Aaron, and dealing with these roadblocks. No wonder you're overwhelmed."

I nodded, a weight pressing down on me. "I thought we were making progress. Every time we step forward, it feels like we're pushed back two."

"Resistance often comes with change. You're challenging the status quo. People like David Prescott and his allies don't want things to transform. They benefit from the way it is."

I stared up, meeting her gaze. "I realize, but it's hard not to believe we're starting a losing battle. Every delay and rumor make it harder to keep everyone motivated."

Chelsea gave a small, reassured smile. "Hope's hardest when the obstacles pile up. Think about what you're fighting for the park, Aaron's campaign. This is bigger than these setbacks. This is about shaping the future of this town."

"It's challenging when you're facing resistance. It appears like we're stuck in a never-ending cycle of problems."

"Sometimes," Chelsea squeezed my hand, "the toughest battles lead to the greatest victories. You're pushing for something that matters, and that's why there's so much pushback."

I took a deep breath, the warmth of the coffee seeping into my bones. Chelsea's words eased some of the tension in my chest. "You're right. I need to remember why we're doing this. The park is a small part of a bigger fight."

She nodded. "The challenges with the playground reflect the larger issues we're up against. We can push through this and make a real difference."

I glanced out the window at the park a few blocks away. "Thanks. I needed this perspective. Sometimes, I lose sight of the bigger picture."

She smiled. "Anytime. You're doing important work, Breanna. Don't forget that."

I nodded, determined. The road ahead wasn't easy, but quitting wasn't an option. Not anymore. Not when we were so close to making a real difference.

Chapter 8

The debate was coming, and Aaron's nervousness grew with every passing day. Every step he took seemed heavier, like the burden of the election sat on his shoulders. He stood before the mirror, adjusting his tie, his brow furrowed.

"Brooks got Prescott's endorsement today," he said, voice tense. "That's not a blow. It's a bomb."

Leaning against the doorway, I watched him. His movements were sharp, not the calm, confident man I was used to seeing. "You can handle him." The knot in my gut wouldn't ease.

His eyes met mine in the mirror. "This debate isn't about me and Brooks anymore. Prescott's endorsement changes everything. People listen when he talks. They believe him."

He was right. His influence ran deep in this town. He rode that wave now, and the polls showed it. The margin was closing fast.

I crossed the room and stood beside him. "You've got the facts. He's lying. You can tear him apart if you stay focused."

Aaron nodded, but the anxiety didn't leave his face. "I don't have to win this evening," he muttered, adjusting his collar again. "I have to knock him out."

The truth of that hit me hard. This debate could turn everything around. Brooks had Prescott's money and his support. Aaron had integrity, but it doesn't always win elections.

I forced myself to speak, to push through the fear gnawing at me. "You've got more than that. You've got the people. They have faith in you. They understand you."

A silence fell between us. I didn't have an answer. The town had been through so much, and now it seemed like the battle wasn't political, it was personal for all of us.

"I don't like this," I admitted, looking down at the floor. "Something appears off about this evening. His being behind Brooks... it looks like a setup."

Aaron looked at me, concern flickering in his eyes. "What do you mean?"

I shook my head. "I don't understand. Maybe it's intuition. He doesn't back someone without expecting something in return. He plays dirty. What if he comes out swinging with something?"

Aaron's chin tensed. "I'll have to be prepared for anything."

The night stretched before us, full of uncertainty. I realized what he was against, and it wasn't him. Prescott represented corruption, power, and a town controlled for far too long.

I looked at him, my heart pounding. "Don't play his game. Stay true to what got you here."

He nodded, his resolve hardening. "I won't stoop to their level. I'll be ready."

He kissed my forehead, and I closed my eyes, holding onto that moment because on the other side of tonight, the battle began. A campaign, a debate, and the truth waiting to be exposed.

The drive to the studio appeared longer than it was. The streets were quiet, yet Aaron and I felt no stress. I could spot his grip tightening on the steering wheel, his knuckles white against the leather. The radio played, but neither of us noticed it. My thoughts circled back to Prescott, Brooks, and the night ahead. It felt like we were heading into something bigger than a debate.

I stole a glance at Aaron. His focused face held something else, something unsaid. I wanted to reach out and tell him it would be okay, but I wasn't sure it would be. Not with Prescott looming over everything.

As we pulled into the studio parking lot, a crowd was already gathering near the entrance. Reporters, campaign aides, and their staff. Aaron adjusted his tie and took a deep breath. Despite his earlier nervousness, he appeared calmer now.

A staff person rushed over to greet us. "We're set inside. You're on in twenty"

"Good. Let's make sure we are ready.".

I followed Aaron into the building. The hallway lights were too bright, throwing long shadows on the walls. The studio was alive—from the microphones being adjusted, sound levels checked, cameras positioned. So, the tension in there was thick, almost electric.

A few of Aaron's supporters approached us, offering handshakes and words of encouragement. "We're behind you, Aaron. You've got this."

He nodded, his smile tight. "Thanks. I appreciate it."

We pushed through the crowd toward his prep room, but my mind was elsewhere. Should I still cover this? The question twisted in my gut. Tonight, I wasn't just a journalist, I was his wife. And the lines between the two blurred more with every step.

Inside, Thomas was waiting. "You ready?"

Aaron gave a quick nod, but I saw the tension in his eyes. "As ready as I'll ever be." Then he glanced at me. "Any updates on Prescott?"

I shook my head. "Nothing new, but I've got a bad hunch about this evening. Brooks has Prescott's backing, and it's going to show."

He frowned, his jaw tightening. "We'll handle it. He's got this."

I wanted to believe him, but the pit in my belly told me otherwise.

He looked at me as we neared the stage, his hand brushing mine. "No matter what happens tonight, I'm glad you're here."

I squeezed his hand, trying to hide the unease I noticed. "We're in this together."

He gave me a small smile, but it didn't reach his eyes. He turned, walking toward the lights of the debate stage.

Air in the pre-room felt heavier than it should have been. And Aaron adjusted his tie for the third time today. His eyes flicked to the mirror, back to me, and then to the floor.

Aaron whispered, glancing at me, "I don't grasp how you're holding it together."

"I'm not," I admitted. My chest tightened with every breath. This debate, Prescott, the scandal. I could feel something was off.

He looked at me, his face set, but I could notice the worry in his eyes. "What do you mean?"

"I don't understand. This whole thing... Prescott endorsing him. The timing. They're waiting to pull the rug out from under us."

Aaron sighed. "I can't think about him now. I have to focus on tonight. He is my opponent, not the other way around."

"You weren't running this campaign," my frustration edged in. "Thomas was."

He shook his head, his eyes hardening. "If I think like that, and I've already lost."

I wanted to argue, to push back, but I couldn't. He was correct. The journalist in me, the part that realized what he was capable of, kept whispering that something wasn't right. "I'm supposed to report on this," I said, experiencing the conflict rise inside me. "If I break the story on him. It might destroy him, but it can also destroy you. And I don't want that."

Aaron stopped, his eyes meeting mine. "I understand."

Silence stretched between us, and I was not too fond of it. I hated I couldn't separate my roles as a journalist, wife, and supporter. They were all tangled up in Prescott's web, and I was stuck in the middle.

"I don't realize how to balance this," I admitted. "I want to take him down, but what if it backfires on you?"

He crossed the room in two quick strides, his hands resting on my shoulders. "Breanna, you have to do what's right. If that means taking down Prescott, then you do it. I'll handle whatever comes."

"What if I'm incorrect?" I asked. "What if I ruin everything?"

His grip tightened, his gaze steady. "You're not wrong. You've never been wrong about him."

I closed my eyes, leaning into the warmth of his presence, but the unease didn't leave. The debate loomed. "I can't shake this vibe," I said, pulling back.

The event was hours away, but resembled something far bigger and was waiting beyond it. Something we couldn't expect, but I knew it was there. And so I warned him. "Be careful."

He smiled, but it didn't reach his eyes. "Always."

I saw him go. The debate was his fight, but Prescott's shadow loomed over everything. I wasn't sure how long I could stay on both sides of this battle.

I sat in the corner of the prep room, watching Aaron adjust his jacket again. He focused, but I noticed the tension in his jaw. Tonight was the last hurdle.

My phone vibrated. I check the caller id, *Samantha*.

I stepped into the hallway. "Hello?"

Her voice came through, cutting through the murmur of the studio. "Breanna, I've got something. It's big. Prescott's tied to more than shady deals. There's evidence of direct bribes to city officials."

"What about campaign contributions to Brooks? Any evidence?"

"There's a wire transfer from Prescott to his account. Fifty thousand dollars. It went through today."

I experienced my heart skipping. "Today? That's the same day he endorsed him."

"I'll email you the files now."

We'd been chasing this for weeks—proof that could bring down Prescott. The timing couldn't have been worse.

"You're sure?" I asked, my voice tight.

"Positive," she said. "Bank records. Transfers linked to Prescott's accounts. It'll blow the whole thing open."

I leaned against the wall. "I release it now. They'll think it's a political move. It destroys Aaron's chances."

"I understand. Waiting means giving him more time with his endorsement. This could shift everything."

I rubbed my forehead, sensing the pressure building. "I can't do that to Aaron. Not right before the debate."

She sighed. "This is bigger than the campaign. It's the town. It's the corruption you've been trying to expose."

I detected her frustration, but she was correct. I glanced back toward the prep room. He stood with Thomas, nodding at something he said, unaware of the storm brewing outside the door.

"If I wait, Brooks may win. With Prescott's support, who understands what will happen to the community?"

"If you don't?"

"If I don't... I risk losing Aaron's trust. The voters might view it as a desperate move, even if it's true."

The hallway engulfed me. Should I release the story now, risking everything we've built?

"I can't do this to him," I whispered, more to myself than to Samantha. "Not tonight."

"Breanna, Prescott's influence is already out there. You don't know what they're planning."

I closed my eyes, and the decision tore at me. "I'll wait."

She didn't argue. She grasped what this meant. "Alright. This will come out."

I ended the call and slipped the phone back into my pocket, my stomach churning. I walked back into the room, my mind spinning with what I'd chosen to bury.

Aaron looked up, offering me a small smile. "Everything okay?"

I forced myself to nod. "Yeah," I said, though the words were like a lie.

He stepped closer, straightening his tie. "I need to be at my best tonight. This debate... it's everything."

I nodded again, my chest tightening. He did not know what I was holding back.

"I believe in you," I said.

I witnessed him go, knowing that my choice would change everything, whether I was ready for it. The consequences of holding back would ripple through this night, and the debate. I hadn't prepared myself to face them yet. Not now.

Aaron walked onto the stage, and my decision hung heavy over me.

Aaron stood at the podium, shoulders squared, but I could notice the tension in his posture. Brooks' eyes darted toward Aaron, smirking like he realized something Aaron didn't. The moderator welcomed the audience and outlined the debate format, but I focused on Aaron.

Brooks started with his usual polished tone, playing the part of the concerned candidate. "It's time for fresh leadership," he said. "We can't keep repeating the same mistakes." Brooks' gaze slid toward Aaron, a subtle jab meant to unsettle him.

Aaron's response came measured, but his voice had an edge. "We don't desire empty promises. We need action, and I've shown that through community projects and proper engagement."

Prescott's endorsement loomed over the debate, casting a shadow neither of us could shake. Brooks leaned into it, letting the support hang like a loaded weapon. Prescott's association with him was already clear.

My stomach twisted. I had the information and proof of his corruption, but I held it. Was that a mistake? I wasn't sure anymore. I saw him throw another veiled comment, this time more directly.

"Of course, some people might talk about change," Brooks said, his smile thin. "When questionable sources fund you, can we trust it?"

Aaron's jaw tightened. I gripped the edge of my seat, knowing he was baiting him. Aaron took a breath, his voice steady but strained.

"My campaign is about transparency and accountability. I've never hidden where my support comes from."

The moderator shifted the focus to policy, but the damage was done. I could detect it in his eyes. He held back frustration, but acknowledged the pressure was mounting.

Aaron hadn't finished speaking. He leaned forward, his eyes locked on him. "Can we trust someone who doesn't have the backing of this town's real influential businessmen?"

He didn't flinch. "I don't need their money to represent this town. I'm here for the people, not special interests."

Another round of applause followed, but it felt hollow. The tension in the room was palpable. I swallowed hard, knowing I had the key to shifting this debate. Maybe the entire campaign, but at what cost?

Aaron spoke again, his voice rising a notch. "We've all seen what happens when power goes unchecked. I'm not here to protect those who've benefited from backroom deals."

Brooks' eyes narrowed. He realized Aaron was talking about Prescott without saying his name. The air felt electric, as if everyone was waiting.

I sat there, my heart pounding, wondering if holding the story was the right call. It was about to surface. He stood tall behind the podium, his hands gripping the edges, knuckles white. The room was quiet, save for the shuffling of the moderators' papers and the occasional audience murmur. His eyes scanned the room, but I could tell his focus was on one thing: Brooks.

Brooks leaned into his microphone, his smile easy, and practiced. "I think we can all agree that having the correct connections is important," he said. "David Prescott's support for my campaign shows that I have the trust of those who understand how to get things done."

Aaron shifted. It was subtle, but I could observe the tension ripple through his shoulders. Brooks had just mentioned the one thing we had hoped to avoid—his looming shadow.

I felt my stomach tighten. The decision to hold back the Prescott story gnawed at me. Could I sit through this debate, knowing it may swing things if I released what I had? At what cost? The room seemed smaller, the air thicker.

He cleared his throat, his voice calm but steady. "This election isn't about your associates. It's about who you serve. Our community needs actual change, not more deals behind closed doors."

Brooks's smile flickered, but he kept his composure. "You talk about change. What have you done to make it happen? The voters deserve more than empty promises."

Aaron's eyes flashed, but his tone controlled. "I've worked alongside the people. The park revitalization project is the beginning. We're building something for everyone, not for the few."

He chuckled, leaning back. "We all understand projects like that don't get done without the right people backing them. That's why Prescott believes in my vision."

The words landed like a punch. My pulse quickened as I clenched the edge of my chair. Aaron had done everything to distance himself from Prescott's influence, but here it was, being thrown in his face. I was sitting on the story that might turn this entire debate upside down.

Aaron's voice broke through my thoughts. "I believe in earning trust, not buying it," he said, his gaze fixed on Brooks. "Our community deserves better than influence peddling."

"Influence gets things done."

The crowd murmured. Aaron's jaw tightened, and he glanced my way for a second, searching for reassurance. I gave him a slight nod, but inside, I was spinning. What if holding back the story was a mistake? What if this debate was the moment we lost?

Aaron dug in. "What gets things done, Martin, is hard work. It's standing with the people, not hiding behind friends."

Brooks didn't flinch. "You can stand with them all you want. Without the resources, what can you accomplish?"

I bit my lip, sensing the tension between them build. This wasn't just about the debate anymore—it was about breaking free from Prescott's grip without getting buried.

I kept checking the clock. The story was growing by the minute. I understood we were at a crossroads. Prescott would be right behind him if he gained more ground, and the damage might be irreversible. If I released it now, would it expose the truth or make Aaron look a desperate candidate who'd use a scandal to win?

The debate ended in a mix of applause and murmurs. Aaron held his ground until the last minute, his voice steady as he gave his closing remarks. Brooks had landed his points. The crowd seemed torn, some nodding at Aaron's words while others leaned toward him.

I stood at the side of the stage, my stomach twisted in knots. He stepped down, his face tight, eyes scanning the crowd before meeting mine. We didn't need to speak. The tension between us was palpable.

Ride home was quiet as the dark roads stretching ahead, our engine's sounds the only noise in the quiet night. Aaron gripped the wheel, his knuckles pale under the dashboard light. I stared out the window, my thoughts racing, Prescott-story still on my mind.

He broke the silence. "He's got Prescott. They think that's enough to win."

I glanced at him, noting the frustration etched on his face. "They're banking on that endorsement carrying them all the way," I said. "You held your own. You showed people what you stand for."

Aaron's jaw tightened; his eyes still focused on the road. "It doesn't matter if Prescott's pulling the strings. People trust money and power more than integrity."

I didn't have an answer to that. He wasn't wrong. I couldn't shake the impression that holding back the story had been a mistake.

We drove for a few more minutes, the weight of the night settling over us. I could detect his disappointment seeping into the air, his shoulders heavy with the effort of keeping it all together.

My phone rang, shattering the quiet. I reached for it, and the screen lit up with Ashley's name. "It's Ashley," I glanced at him. He nodded, his gaze still fixed ahead.

Something seemed wrong when I detected her voice on the other end. It was weaker and softer than usual, and it sounded like she was struggling to catch her breath.

"I viewed the debate," she said, pausing for a second. "Aaron held his ground. Tell him congratulations."

I blinked, trying to process her tone. "Thanks, I will," I replied, my voice faltering. "You sound... are you okay?"

There was a long pause. I could listen to her shifting like she was adjusting herself. "I'm in the hospital. It got worse... faster than doctors expected."

The words hit me like a punch. "What? Since when?"

"A couple of days," she said, her voice strained but steady. "I didn't want to say anything before. You've had enough to deal with."

I gripped the phone tighter, my mind racing. "Ashley, you should have told me."

"I understand. I didn't want to distract you. You've got so much on your plate. The investigation... Aaron's campaign..."

Her words trailed off, leaving a silence that appeared too heavy.

"I'm coming to visit you," I said, thinking about the fastest route to the hospital.

"Would you?" she asked, her voice fragile but grateful. "I'd like that."

I nodded, though she couldn't notice it. "I'll be there soon."

Aaron glanced at me, concern flashing as he caught my expression. I ended the call, trying to steady my breath.

"Ashley's in the hospital," I said.

His eyes widened. "What happened?"

"She said little." I paused, my chest tight. "She asked me to visit her."

Aaron reached for my hand, his grip firm. "Go. I'll manage things here."

I squeezed his hand in return, but the weight of everything was pressing down. The campaign, the investigation, and now Ashley... It was all crashing in at once.

Chapter 9

What Samantha told me on the call, I couldn't get that out of my mind. The wire transfer from Prescott into Brooks' account wasn't a minor detail. It was explosive. Sharing it... I didn't understand if it would hurt Aaron more than it helped. It seemed too calculated, too close to the election. People would say it was a political attack, a desperate move to sabotage Brooks.

I stared at my phone, Samantha's message still fresh in my inbox, waiting for me to decide. We had proof of Prescott's reach. But if I exposed it, would it help Aaron or destroy him?

Whatever the answer, I had to let him know about the information Samantha gave me last night.

Speaking of Aaron, he was sitting at the kitchen table, papers in front of him. He stared up when I entered the room, his eyes tired but focused. The campaign was wearing him down, but he wasn't exhausted. Not yet.

"I need to talk to you." My voice was quiet as I sat across from him.

Aaron asked, his brows furrowing. "What's going on?"

I took a breath, pushing the phone toward him. "Samantha found something. It's big."

He looked at the screen, reading the message, his face tightening with every word. "Fifty thousand?" he said. "From Prescott, straight to Brooks?"

I nodded, experiencing the knot in my stomach tighten. "It's real. She has the proof. I might disclose it."

He leaned forward, his hands gripping the table's edge. "You release this now, and it'll seem like an attack. Brooks and Prescott will spin it like we're desperate."

"I understand. But if we don't, Prescott will keep backing him and we'll lose."

He stared at me, his eyes hard. "Is this about winning—or exposing the truth?"

I hesitated. "Both. Prescott is bad, and people need to know it. But... yes, it can help you."

He rubbed his temples, the stress clear in his movements. "People will say we're playing dirty."

"Maybe," I said, trying to hold his eye contact. "It's a fact. I'm not fabricating anything. I'm not pulling something out of thin air. This is the truth."

He looked away, his jaw clenched. He understood this may change everything, but realized how it can backfire.

"I don't want to win like that. I don't want to use this to destroy him."

"It's not about him. It's about what Prescott's doing to this town."

Aaron sat there, his hands still gripping the table's edge.

"You think this is the right move?" he asked, his voice quiet.

"I think... it's the truth." My heart was pounding. "I think people deserve to be aware of who they vote for."

He peered at me, searching my face for something, some reassurance. "If we do this, we do it clean. No spinning, no games."

I nodded. "The facts."

Aaron sighed, standing up and pacing the kitchen. "Alright. Release it. Let the town see who Prescott is."

I watched him, the anxiety in the room not easing even though we'd decided. This wasn't the victory I wanted. It didn't seem like a win, but it was necessary. Now, there was no turning back.

The morning after the story aired, the community appeared different. It appeared as if a line had divided the community, separating those who believed from those who didn't. The story had hit hard, but not in the way I'd hoped. Aaron's hadn't gained the traction I thought it would. It left a trail of doubt.

I sat at the news desk, watching the phones light up in the control room. Callers flooded in, some furious, others thankful. Through the glass, I could detect the mix of anger and support. A division existed among the town's residents.

As soon as my shift ended, I headed straight to Aaron's office. Aaron was standing before the whiteboard, reviewing numbers with Thomas. His face appeared tense, more tired than usual.

He looked at me when I walked in, his eyes scanning for signs of how I was holding up. I forced a smile, but we both recognized this wasn't the outcome we expected.

"How's it looking?" I asked.

Thomas sighed, stepping back from the board. "Mixed. Some people are with us, but... there's a backlash. They think we timed it for the campaign."

Aaron turned, his jaw tight. "They think it was a smear."

I swallowed, experiencing the tightening knot in my stomach. "The rest?"

He rubbed his temples. "They believe it, but wait to watch how he responds. He hasn't said a word yet."

I could feel the tension in the air, heavy. This was what I feared. The story had exposed Prescott's corruption, but at what cost? The town's division put Aaron's integrity at risk.

"I knew this would be risky," Aaron said. "I didn't think it would hit us this hard."

I stepped closer, placing a hand on his arm. "We did the right thing."

Aaron stared at me, his eyes searching for reassurance. "Did we? Did we make it worse?"

The room fell silent. Thomas shifted, clearing his throat. "We can still persevere through this. It's not over."

Aaron nodded, but I could see the doubt creeping in. "No. It's not over."

We stood there, the decision hanging between us. The story divided the town, and now we must repair the damage.

Outside, the sun was setting, casting long shadows across the street. I gazed out the window, watching as people passed by. Some glanced at the office, others didn't, but the air felt charged, like it was waiting for something to happen.

I turned back to Aaron. "We'll get through this."

He gave me a slight nod, but the unease in his eyes didn't ease.

The rest of the evening passed in a blur of strategy meetings and phone calls. The campaign team was scrambling to handle the fallout, trying to regain control of the narrative. The division was clear, and it was growing.

At night, we found ourselves alone in the office. The energy from earlier had fizzled out, leaving it quiet.

"I don't know if we can fix this," Aaron said as he moved closer to me and sat in his chair.

I sat down across from him, meeting his gaze. "You're fighting for the right reasons. That's what matters."

He leaned back, his eyes tired. "I hope people see that."

I reached, taking his hand. "They will. This isn't the end."

Aaron's grip tightened around mine, but the doubt lingered. The story's aftermath had shifted everything in ways we hadn't expected. What was once a calculated risk now felt like wildfire, spreading beyond our control. We couldn't ignore the weight of public opinion and how it rocked between support and suspicion. The air was uncertain, but we both knew sitting still wasn't an option.

Aaron looked at me. "We've got to get ahead of this. The story's out, and now they're coming after us."

I nodded, all pressing on my chest. "Prescott and Brooks are planting stories. People are believing we did this to hurt him in the polls."

His jaw tightened, and his gaze lingered on the flyer a moment longer than necessary, but he didn't say a word. His determination was one reason I fell in love with him. He was not the kind to back down when things got challenging.

"We need to shift the focus," I said, leaning forward. "People have to see this isn't about politics."

He shook his head. "That's hard to do. Prescott has the money and the connections to sway public opinion. He's using everything against us."

I heard the exhaustion in his voice, but there was something else, too—a flicker of doubt. The pressure was getting to him, and I didn't know how much more he could take.

"We can't let him control the complete story. You've always stood for transparency. We need to double down."

He glanced at me, his jaw tight. "How do we do that without making this look like a desperate move?"

I paused, thinking it over. "We remind people what you've done for the community. The park project, the town halls, and the outreach. Show them you're not a politician. You're one of them."

Aaron nodded. "We must prove we are not like Prescott. I'm fighting for something bigger than an election."

"We have to regain their trust." I met his eyes. His attacks aren't as effective as they seem.

He stood, pacing the room. I saw his mind working through the details, searching for control. He stopped, looking at me with renewed determination.

"I'll hold a press conference," he said. "No scripted speeches. Just talking to the people. No more hiding behind political advisors."

I smiled, feeling a flicker of hope. "That's what they need to see. You, standing for what's right."

He reached for my hand, squeezing it.

"We're in this together," I said, the knot in my chest easing a little.

He nodded, his shoulders straightening.

The attacks started, subtle whispers woven into news segments and articles. At first, it seemed like a coincidence. The headlines became sharper, more pointed. The morning after the exposé, I felt the shift in the air. Prescott had mobilized his network. The smear against us had begun.

I sat in the living room, scrolling through the articles on my phone. My stomach twisted with each headline. "*Scandal or Smear? Aaron Robert's Campaign Under Fire*" read one. Another questioned the timing: "*Convenient Corruption Claims: Is This Just Politics as Usual?*"

He came in from the kitchen, his face tight with frustration. "They're saying we fabricated the whole thing. We're using this to tear Brooks down before the election."

I nodded, unable to pull my eyes away from the screen. "Prescott and Brooks are spinning the narrative. People are buying into it."

Aaron's jaw clenched, his hands gripping the back of the chair before him. "I should've known Prescott wouldn't go down without a fight. He's not defending Brooks. He's protecting himself."

I looked at Aaron. "We're losing control of the story. They're framing it as a desperate move on your part. Like you needed something to shift the issues."

Aaron stopped and turned to face me. "We've worked too hard for this. I will not let David's lies undo everything." His voice was steady, but I saw the strain in his eyes.

I stood and crossed the room to stand beside him. "What do we do now? We push back too hard. It might seem like we're trying to cover something up."

He sighed, running a hand through his hair. "We focus on what matters. The community. We battle his media war, and we'll never win. We stick to the facts, stay above the mud."

I nodded, knowing he was right. Prescott's reach was vast. His allies controlled much of the local press, and their planting stories were gaining traction.

The phone rang, cutting through the tension in the room. I answered, bracing myself. It was one producer from the station. "Breanna, we've got a problem. Prescott's people are pushing back hard on the exposé. They're accusing us of running a political hit piece."

My chest tightened. "What are they saying?"

"They've been feeding stories to other outlets, questioning the legitimacy of the evidence you uncovered. They're trying to turn it into a political scandal, claiming you used your position to sway the election."

I glanced at Aaron, who was watching me. "What's the station's stance on this?"

"We're standing by the story, but the pressure's mounting. We need to be sure there's nothing they can twist further."

I hung up, feeling dread. He stepped closer, his eyes searching mine. "What is it?"

"Prescott's pushing harder than we thought. They're questioning my integrity, too. Saying I used the expose things to manipulate elections."

Aaron's expression darkened. "Of course they are. They'll do anything to make us appear like the bad guys."

I swallowed hard. "This is getting ugly."

I nodded, though my mind raced with all the possibilities. David was not after the campaign. He was after our reputation, our credibility. I wasn't sure how much we held the line.

Aaron's grip was tight around my hand. "We stand our ground."

Aaron rubbed his temples, his face etched with concern. "And we have more evidence. Which we can release to turn the tide, but it could also backfire."

I glanced at the documents. "Do we use it to hit back hard or take a slower pace?"

He leaned back in his chair, his gaze fixed on the ceiling. "Going on the offensive side might expose more of Prescott's corruption, but it risks escalating the situation. We may alienate potential supporters and give him more ammunition to attack us."

I sighed, trying to steady my thoughts. "We let him define the narrative. He's already framing us as the villains. We need to counter that somehow."

Aaron's hands clenched into fists. "Every time we try to fight back, it feels like we're losing ground. His network is relentless. They've got the media on their side."

I picked up a document. "We go all out. We could make things worse. We've seen how people react to the accusations. Some believe it's a smear campaign."

The room was silent for a moment, the only sound the distant hum of the city outside. Aaron straightened, his shoulders stiffening as he exhaled slowly, the lines on his face deepening with each passing second.

"We need to think about the long term. If we go on the offensive, we risk further damage to your campaign. If we don't, we might lose everything we've worked for."

Aaron stood and walked to the window, his shoulders tense. He peered out at the street below, where life continued. "Release some proof to reveal we're sincere, but not everything. Make a powerful statement without going on the attack."

I felt cautious optimism. "We can show we're fighting back. Although we've to avoid escalating the situation further."

He turned back to me, his expression softening. "Be careful. Every move counts now."

I met his gaze, feeling the decision to settle between us. "Let's prepare the selected evidence and ensure it's clear, but not too explosive."

He nodded in agreement. "We'll handle this step by step. One mistake now cost us everything."

We began sorting through the documents, our actions deliberate. We examined each piece of evidence and then wrote a statement. The choice hung over us, but we tried to balance the need for action with the risks involved.

They made the choice, and the town seemed to fracture further. Aaron's supporters rallied around him with renewed enthusiasm, holding signs and chanting in front of his veterinarian's office.

Aaron paced back and forth while I leaned against the desk. His hands were moving in sharp gestures as he spoke. "We knew it would get worse, but this... this is something else. I thought we managed it... Now? I'm not so sure."

The door to the office creaked open, and Gretchen, one of our campaign staff, stepped in. She wore a grim, determined expression. "I've been out there talking to people. The divide is real, and it's growing. We need to address it before it gets worse."

His expression was weary, but resolute. "Then what should we do?"

Gretchen glanced out the window at the protests and counter-protests below. "Perhaps we can bridge the gap by showing our intentions---that we're for everyone, not just us."

"That's great." I thanked her for the opinion. Then I turned to Aaron, my heart heavy with the weight of our choices. "We're committed to fairness, not winning a battle."

He took a deep breath, his shoulders squared with resolve. "You're right. We need to be the ones to bring people back to the table."

The phone rang, slicing through the thick silence. He answered, "Hello?" His face tightened as he listened, his brows knitting together.

I watched him, my anxiety mounting with each passing second. Aaron's grip on the receiver was white-knuckled. He hung up. His expression was grim.

"We've got a problem," he said, rubbing his temple.

"What happened?" I asked, my heart pounding.

"The legal team from Brook's camp is threatening a lawsuit," he said. "They're accusing us of libel and demanding a retraction."

I swallowed hard, the news settling over me. "This is getting out of hand. It's not about public opinion anymore."

Aaron nodded, his jaw set. "I know. We're not facing a smear campaign; we're staring down a legal battle."

I paced the room, trying to make sense of the situation. "What do we do now? If we back down, it will look like we're admitting defeat."

He ran a hand through his hair, frustrated. "We can't back down. If we do, Prescott and Brooks win. We also need to be careful. They might use it against us in court if we push too hard."

The door gently open, and Gretchen entered, her face reflecting the seriousness of what was happening. "Do we have a plan?"

"Brook's and Prescott are trying to discredit us. We can't afford to give him more ammunition."

She nodded, her face lined with concern. "We can prove we acted in good faith. It might help us in court."

I joined in, feeling the pressure intensify. "We should address the public. If they see us fighting against David's tactics, it might sway opinion in our favor."

Aaron took a deep breath, his resolve hardening. "I'll meet with our legal team. We are prepared for whatever David throws at us."

Gretchen's gaze was steady. "I'll work on organizing a press conference. We need to control the story."

The reality of the situation hit me hard. We were no longer reporters and candidates; we were now part of a high-stakes game.

Scattered papers covered my desk, reflecting the chaos in my mind. I tapped at my keyboard, trying to organize the mounting evidence. The media was relentless.

The door opened, and Aaron strode in, his brow furrowed. He slammed a stack of papers onto the desk. "Prescott's retaliation is getting constant."

I looked up, tired eyes meeting his. "I've seen. His team is everywhere, and the public backlash is hitting hard."

He rubbed the back of his neck, frustration clear in his posture. "What's the plan?"

"I'm working on strengthening the investigation," I said, pulling out the latest documents. "We've had new leads."

Aaron's look sharpened. "How do we make this work against the tide of opposition?"

"We have to stay focused," I said, pushing a folder toward him. "And hit back harder."

Aaron flipped through the folder, his expression growing more resolute. "Is there enough here to make a difference?"

"Yes. We've got solid evidence. It's risky, but it's our best shot."

He exhaled, his shoulders sagging with the decision. "It will get worse before it gets better."

I nodded, feeling the burden of our choices. "That's a risk we have to take."

He met my eye contact, determination hardening his features. "Alright. Let's do this. We'll move ahead forward and face whatever comes."

I felt a surge of resolve. Despite the mounting pressure, stepping back wasn't an option. We had to keep moving, no matter how high the stakes were.

My phone buzzed, breaking the silence. Ashley's name flashed on the screen. I answered quickly, trying to keep my voice calm.

"Breanna," her voice was clear but strained. "I'm glad you picked up."

I adjusted my position, leaning closer to the phone. "Ashley, what's going on?"

She and I talked for a few minutes. I was concentrating on the information she was telling me.

"Are you sure about this?"

"Yes," she replied. "I've reviewed the documents. They're solid. It would be best if you acted fast, though. Prescott will fight back."

"Okay." My mind was racing with the implications. "I'll take it from here. Thank you."

I gazed at Aaron. His concern is apparent.

"Ashley has concrete evidence against Prescott."

Aaron's eyes narrowed. "This is our chance to hit back. How soon can we use this information?"

"I'm ready to take it to the authorities. We need to be strategic about this, though. He will not take this lying down."

We set to work to face the next phase of our effort.

Chapter 10

The evidence was undeniable. There were wire transfers, fake companies, and bribes. Everything pointed to Prescott. It was enough to bring David Prescott down for good. I sensed the pressure in my chest. The election was days away. Aaron was ahead in the polls, but this wasn't about winning.

I picked up the phone and dialed Detective Ruiz. We'd worked together on a few stories before and he knew I didn't deal in half-truths. My fingers tapped against the desk as I waited for him to answer.

"Breanna?" Ruiz's voice came through, familiar and constant.

"Hi, Ruiz. I've got something big. It's Prescott."

The silence stretched for a moment. I pictured him sitting back, processing. He wasn't a name in this town. He was a storm, a force of nature waiting to collide with the pillars of our community.

"What've you got?"

"A wire transfer. Fifty thousand dollars straight from Prescott into Brooks' campaign account."

There was a pause, "Are you saying—"

"It's a bribe, Ruiz. A clear connection."

I listened to the rustle of papers on his end. "You're sure about this?"

I pushed the folder across my desk like he was sitting beside me. "I've got proof. Paper trails. It's clean."

He grunted, thinking. "This is explosive, Breanna."

"That's why it needs to happen now. This doesn't come out. Both Prescott and Brooks win."

"Aaron loses," Ruiz said.

I reclined back in my chair, staring at the documents that would turn Centerville upside down. "This isn't about him. This is about our community."

He sighed. "You comprehend what that'll be like. Prescott's people will spin it."

"I'm not fabricating evidence. I'm handing you facts."

"Alright. Send me what you've got."

"Sure. But have to leave as I'm about to go on air with it all," I said, standing.

"You're walking a fine line here, Breanna," Ruiz warned. "Careful, it doesn't backfire."

I ended the call and looked at the papers scattered across my desk. He was powerful, but this was bigger than him. It had to be.

I gathered the files, packed them into a folder, and headed to the station. The whole way there, my mind swirled with doubts. Would the town believe this additional evidence? Would they view it as a last-minute play by Aaron's team?

As I walked into the studio, I noticed the energy shift. Eyes followed me, curious, some nervous. They understood something was coming. My producer, Connie, gave me a look but said nothing as I handed her the papers.

My pulse was stable. The cameras clicked on, and hot and bright lights flooded the room.

"Tonight, we break a story that affects the future of our town," he said, looking into the lens. "Evidence of bribery, corruption, and illegal campaign donations. Centerville resident and well-renowned businessman David Prescott was behind all of it."

I didn't flinch. Didn't blink. The words came out like punches, each one landing with force. The teleprompter rolled, and the facts came out through the telecast.

When I finished, the studio was silent. No one moved, and the air was thick. Connie handed me a cup of water, but I didn't drink it. My hand shook, holding it. I wasn't afraid.

I walked outside, the cool air slapping my face, clearing my thoughts. I checked my phone. I had a dozen messages already. Ruiz had texted me. *We're moving on Prescott.*

I let out a breath I hadn't realized I was holding. I headed toward Aaron's campaign office, hoping the news would affect like it should. Aaron stood by the whiteboard, reviewing numbers with Thomas. He glanced up, his eyes tired but sharp.

"How'd it go?" he asked, crossing his arms.

"It's out there. Prescott's finished." I handed him the folder of evidence. He thumbed through it, a furrow deepening in his brow.

"Polls are shifting," Thomas added, not looking away from the board. "We're ahead, but his people will spin this hard."

He flipped through the documents. His jaw clenched. "This sealed it," he said. "It blew everything up."

I watched him. "We couldn't sit on it."

"I understand," he said. "People are already calling it a conspiracy."

"They'll realize the facts." I hoped I sounded more confident.

Thomas tapped a marker against the board. "We're getting pushback from Brooks' camp. His financials are clean on the surface, but there's more here. We're digging."

I stood straighter. "What do you mean?"

He turned to us, crossing his arms. "Brooks accepted money from Prescott, and there's something deeper. A long-standing connection. Prescott's been quietly funding him for years."

The room fell silent. I exchanged a glance with Aaron. "You think the election's rigged?" I asked, the thought chilling.

"Something's off. Too many coincidences. I'm still tracking it."

Aaron tossed the folder onto the table. "We can't become distracted by conspiracies. We need to focus on what we can prove."

"I'll keep digging," Thomas said. "Be ready for anything."

I left him and Thomas at the campaign office and went home. Prescott's arrest was a victory, but it didn't seem like the end. Something bigger was at play; now, we were all caught in it. The broadcast was over. I sat in the empty newsroom, the lights dimmed, silence filling the space where the buzz of energy had been only an hour before. I had done it. His dirty dealings were out in the open for everyone to witness.

Doubt gnawed at me. I had delivered it, but at what cost? Would they regard it as a desperate move so close to the election? Prescott's people would spin it, make it look like I had orchestrated a political hit. I realized that. Centerville couldn't go forward, with Prescott controlling everything behind the scenes. Now Aaron's effort hung in the balance, and I was the one who'd set the fire.

The door creaked open, the sound pulling me out of my thoughts. Aaron walked in, his face lined with exhaustion. At first, he said nothing; he set his keys down and shrugged off his coat.

I stood, unsure of what to say.

He grabbed a bottle of water from the refrigerator. His movements are slow. "It's out there," he said.

"It had to be," I said, crossing my arms. I kept my voice steady, though a knot twisted in my stomach.

He set the glass down, running a hand over his face. "Prescott's team isn't wasting time. They're already accusing you of staging the whole thing."

I nodded, having expected it. "They were going to attack no matter what. But now, we have them cornered."

Aaron's eyes met mine. He pushed off the counter and started pacing, his movements sharp. "You've put it out there, and now the campaign is on the line.

I didn't flinch. "This wasn't about politics. It was about Prescott's corruption."

He stopped, rubbing his temples. "They don't view it that way, Breanna. People are questioning if this was about the truth or if it was about winning."

I clenched my fists. "You think I did this to win an election? You think I don't care about this town?"

His gaze softened, but the tension remained. "I understand you did it for the right reasons. The timing... it's throwing everything into chaos."

I dropped my arms to my sides, the weight of his words sinking in. "I didn't have a choice. I'd held back. Prescott would've kept digging his claws in deeper. He's already got Brooks in his pocket."

Aaron walked to the window, looking out into the dark. "We're losing ground. Polls are shifting. My team is trying to control the damage, but Prescott's people are working fast."

I stood behind him, my voice softening. "This isn't over. The truth is out there now. It has to. No matter what."

He didn't answer at first, but he kept staring into the distance, his shoulders tense. "I want to believe that," he said. "Right now, I'm not sure what matters anymore."

The silence between us was heavy. The campaign was teetering. Prescott's grip remained stronger than I'd hoped.

Aaron turned, his face tired but resolved. "I'm sorry about earlier. I got a little carried away. It's just that this is getting a lot harder than I thought."

I nodded, knowing he was right. It was getting *hard*, indeed. But we were together in all this. I reassured him, "It's okay. We can do this. Remember, we used to say together, 'I'll stand by you no matter what comes, and we'll face it together'. And that's what we'll do. Together."

For a moment, the weight between us lifted. The uncertainty, the exhaustion, it was still there, but so was something stronger.

The phone buzzed, shaking the quiet of the kitchen. I glanced at the screen, Ruiz. I hadn't realized I'd been holding my breath. My fingers felt stiff as I swiped to answer.

"We've got him," Ruiz said.

My grip tightened. "Prescott?"

"Admitted to the fifty thousand," he said. "We're going through with the booking now."

I stood up, my legs unsteady beneath me. I pressed my free hand against the edge of the counter, grounding myself. "He admitted it?"

"Yeah. Didn't hide it once we showed him the papers." Ruiz's voice didn't waver. Prescott wasn't some low-level crook. This was a man who'd pulled strings in Centerville for years and had always slipped through the cracks until now.

I blinked hard, trying to focus. "The campaign donation? The bribe?"

"He understood we had him. He signed a statement. It's all on record now."

I nodded, though Ruiz couldn't see me. The pressure in my chest loosened a little. "That's it then."

"It's big. His lawyer's already scrambling, but it's happening."

I paced the floor, the sound of my footsteps echoing. Prescott's fall and his connection to Brooks could be more than a win for us. It would be a win for the town.

"The booking?" I asked.

"They're processing him now. It'll hit the papers tomorrow."

I pressed my hand against my forehead, the coolness of my skin grounding me. "Good. It needs to be public."

"It will be. Breanna," he paused, "this isn't over. His team will come after you. They'll spin this."

"I know."

I caught voices in the background, officers moving in and out. Ruiz was in the thick of it. "You did the right thing," he said, his voice softer now.

I nodded, the knot in my throat tightening. "Thanks."

The line clicked off, and I stood there, frozen for a moment. Prescott was going down. The truth was out there. Anything, it pressed harder, heavier.

Aaron glanced up from his spot near the window, his hands resting on a stack of reports. He didn't speak, waiting, reading the tension in my face.

"They're booking him," I said, my voice flat. "Prescott admitted to the fifty thousand. He didn't fight it."

He stood, his expression unreadable. I noticed his shoulders relax slightly.

I shook my head, staring at the phone in my hand. "It should appear like it's done, but it doesn't. He's got people. They'll come after us."

Aaron's jaw clenched. "They'll spin this however they can. His team's already setting the narrative."

"They're going to make it like we pulled this for the election," I said, pacing. "Prescott will not roll over."

"We realized that," Aaron said, stepping closer. "You did what had to be done."

I rubbed my hands over my face, the coolness grounding me. "Did I? The town's going to be divided. His supporters will twist it, say we used this to win."

His gaze softened. He reached out, resting a hand on my arm. "This isn't about winning. You didn't do this for the campaign. You did it because it was right."

I nodded, but the knot in my chest wouldn't loosen. "It's going to become ugly. Worse than it already is."

His eyes darkened. "We'll deal with it. Prescott's influence is fading. We've exposed him. That's what matters."

I grabbed my jacket, noticing the zipper dig into my fingers as I pulled it on. "It should be over, Aaron. It's like it's starting."

He didn't argue. He understood it, too.

The newsroom walls felt too close, the quiet pressing in on me. I pushed the door open and stepped outside. The cool air hit my face, sharp and bracing.

Aaron followed, standing next to me, his presence steady. "Whatever comes, we'll handle it."

I stared at him, knowing he believed it. The intuition in my gut told me this wasn't the end. It was only the beginning.

I stood there, and the tightness in my chest remained. He watched the empty street as the city lights flickered in the distance.

"Let's go home," he said, his voice quieter now.

And we did.

But I didn't realize this was only the calm before the next storm.

I glanced at the clock. It was Election Day. The newsroom buzzed with its usual pre-show activity, but today was anything but normal. I handed Nate the latest news piece, my fingers brushing the cool, glossy paper.

"Got it," Connie said, not bothering to look up from his screen.

I nodded and made my way to the anchor desk. The lights blazed overhead, hotter than yesterday. I adjusted my microphone, willing my hands to stay steady. Since Prescott's arrest, Aaron's election had hung in the balance. And today would determine everything.

I took a slow breath, glanced at the camera, and the teleprompter began rolling. "Good morning, Centerville. I'm Breanna Roberts, and we've got breaking news on this crucial Election Day…"

I kept my tone calm and professional, though every word was heavy. His arrest had caused a ripple. His camp accused us of running a smear campaign. And the town; it seemed like the town was holding its breath.

The camera cut to the latest poll numbers. Aaron's lead still held, but I couldn't shake the sensation that the ground was shifting beneath us. My phone buzzed again, the messages piling up. I ignored it. Now wasn't the time for distractions.

The broadcast ended, and I exhaled, my chest tight. The studio fell quiet. Nate shot me a quick nod of approval, but the encouragement didn't reach me. I forced a smile before heading toward the exit.

Aaron was waiting in the hallway, his arms crossed, worry etched into every line of his face. His tie hung loose like he hadn't slept in days.

"How'd it go?" His voice was strained, though he tried to hide it.

I shrugged, trying to keep my tone. "It's done. It's not over."

His brows knitted together. "What do you mean?"

I leaned against the wall, searching for the right words. "The backlash is building. Prescott's team is all over it. They're saying we're biased, that this is a political hit job. It's getting ugly."

Aaron's jaw clenched. "That swayed voters."

"We've got solid ground, but this narrative they're spinning—it's getting traction. It might hit the polls harder than we expected."

His eyes darkened, the surrounding lines deeper than usual. "What do we do?"

My phone buzzed. I glanced at the screen and froze. It was a text from Ashley. My heart skipped, and a knot formed in my gut. This wasn't good. I hesitated, then read the message:

We need to talk. It's about Prescott. I should have told you sooner.

I froze, the blood rushing in my ears. I reread it, hoping I misunderstood.

Aaron turned from the window, noticing my expression. "What's wrong?"

I couldn't answer. Not yet. My fingers felt numb as I typed back. *What do you mean? What's going on?*

The response came. *I was involved with Prescott's network. I didn't know how deep it went, but I helped him once.*

The words hit like a punch to the gut. My legs weakened. I grabbed the edge of the table to steady myself.

Aaron's eyes darkened as he stepped closer. "Breanna, what is it?"

I shook my head, trying to make sense of it. "Ashley... she's linked to Prescott. She admitted it."

His jaw clenched. "Connected how?"

I scrolled through the rest of her message, the words blurring together. Years ago, they pressured her to help him cover up a scheme. However, she didn't know the full extent of it.

Aaron exhaled, running a hand through his hair. "So, she's been sitting on this the entire time?"

"I guess so," I said, my voice hollow. "She thought she made it right by being here to expose him."

Typing in the message—*I'm coming to the hospital... we need to talk in person*—I hit send and stared at the screen, waiting for a response. Nothing.

I began pacing the station's hallways, my thoughts tangled. A few colleagues passed by, congratulating me on the story. "Good luck to Aaron," they said. "We're behind him."

I forced a smile, nodding as they walked by. "Thanks," I muttered, but my mind was somewhere else. My focus stayed on my phone, waiting for Ashley's reply. I needed answers.

I stared at my phone. My pulse quickened. Aaron's lead was fragile. We were so close. I couldn't afford distractions. Not now.

I glanced at Aaron. He said nothing at first; he watched me with that same steady gaze he always had. Something else in his eyes made the words I wanted to say stick in my throat. I didn't want to leave him with the election hanging in the balance. I had to face Ashley.

"I'll be back soon," I said, though we both knew I couldn't promise that. There was no telling how long this conversation would take or what I would learn.

Aaron stepped forward, resting his hand on my arm. His touch was warm, grounding me for a moment. "Do what you need to," he said. "I'll be here."

I nodded, forcing a small smile. "We'll figure this out."

He said nothing else and slightly nodded before I turned and left.

The drive to the hospital felt more than it should have. The roads were quiet, but my mind wasn't. Ashley's confession had shifted everything. I kept replaying the message, her words twisting in my head. Prescott's network ran more profound than I thought, and now the person I trusted most had been part of it.

I pulled into the parking lot. I took a deep breath, trying to push the doubts aside. I needed to stay focused. The truth was waiting inside, and I had to face it, no matter how much it hurt.

I walked down the sterile, white hallways, the fluorescent lights above buzzing. I found Room 204. I paused outside the door, my hand resting on the handle. I pushed it open.

Ashley lay in the bed, looking pale, her chest rising and falling. She turned her head when she saw me; her face tightening with effort. It looked like that tiny movement took too much from her. I stepped closer, the silence between us thick, weighted by everything left unsaid.

"You came," she said, her voice weak, more than a whisper.

I pulled out a chair and sat down, my fingers nervously tapping on the tabletop. "I needed to hear it from you, Ashley. I'm not sure where to go with this."

Ashley hesitated for a moment, her gaze flickering toward the window before she met my eyes. "I didn't know," she began, her voice quiet. "Not at first. Prescott... he didn't tell me everything. But as things went on, I started putting the pieces together."

I stayed silent, watching her struggle with the words.

"I worked on a story years ago—real estate. It seemed minor at first. I didn't know it then. By the time I knew Prescott was behind it, I had already helped him cover it up." She swallowed hard, her hands tightening together.

I leaned back, the space between us feeling like a chasm. "You were part of his network."

Ashley's eyes flashed with regret. "Not like that. I didn't know what he was doing. When I found out, I couldn't stop it."

My throat felt tight. I had trusted her and her support in this fight. All this time, Prescott had entangled her in his web. "Why didn't you tell me?"

"I thought I could fix it." Her voice trembled. "That's why I came to Centerville and to KBNR and wanted to make things right. I didn't want you to know how I'd messed up."

I stood, pacing the small room, my thoughts spiraling. "How can I trust you now, Ashley? You were part of the very thing I've been trying to expose. You covered for him."

"I didn't know the entire picture, Breanna. When I finally understood everything, it was too late. I was already trapped.

My mind raced. Prescott had caught Ashley in his schemes; how many others had he also caught? How much of the story I'd built around Prescott was true? Who else had been lying?

I crossed my arms, my back to her. "I don't know if I can believe you. You should've told me."

Her voice broke behind me. "I didn't want to lose your trust. I knew you'd find out, eventually."

I turned, facing her again. "I need to rethink everything now, Ashley. This changes how I see all of it."

She didn't argue. Her silence was heavy, filled with guilt.

I rubbed my temples, trying to gather my thoughts. If someone manipulated her, they manipulated others as well. Prescott's influence reached further than I realized, and the election was now tainted in my mind. My investigation, I thought I knew about his corruption, felt like quicksand.

I stared at her one last time, unable to hide the hurt. "I don't know if I can ever trust you again."

The door behind me creaked open. Olivia stepped into the room, her face surprised when she saw me.

"Breanna?" Her voice was full of confusion.

I turned, as confused as she was. "Olivia?"

Ashley's breathing hitched, her hand trembling as she reached for hers. The change in her eyes was subtle, but unmistakable fear, or maybe guilt. It was hard to say.

I waited, the silence stretching between us, until she finally broke it. Her voice was barely more than a whisper, she said, "I didn't... I didn't tell you." She looked away for a moment, as though searching for the right words. "She's my daughter."

The words hung in the air, heavy and unexpected. I stared at Ashley, then at her, who looked as stunned as I felt. We had met at the community cleanup and worked side by side, never knowing this. My mind spun as I tried to piece together everything that had unraveled before me.

She stepped closer, her eyes darting between me and her mother. "What is going on?"

I stood there, unsure of what to said. She looked at Ashley, her eyes wide with shock, trying to process the truth her mother had dropped. I couldn't move, couldn't think. This changed everything, and I didn't know how to respond.

I ran my hand through my hair. I opened my mouth to speak when my phone buzzed, breaking the silence.

I pulled it from my pocket and saw Samantha's name on the screen. My stomach tightened. I glanced at Ashley and Olivia, then answered. "Samantha?"

Her voice came through, tense and urgent. "Breanna, you need to hear this. It's about Prescott."

I walked out into the hallway, needing space from the tension inside the room. "What is it?"

"We found something. It's big. Prescott's real identity—he's David Fredrick, Chris Fredrick's son. The cattle rancher we put away."

The air left the room as I stopped in my tracks. "David Prescott... is Fredrick's son? I can see it now, the same bright blue eyes that can be so inviting and simultaneously so cold."

"Yes," Samantha said, her words sharp, direct. "He changed his name after his father's conviction. It's personal. His whole vendetta—this campaign, it's all revenge."

I leaned against the wall, my heart racing. It made sense. He wasn't after power. He had been coming for me all along.

Samantha's voice cut through my thoughts. "We need to act now. This information changes everything."

I turned back and walked into Ashley's hospital room, where Ashley and Olivia sat, their truth unraveling. My mind reeled, trying to connect all the pieces. "I can't worry about this right now. I have to get back to Aaron and his party."

It all collided with Ashley's confession, Olivia's presence, and now this bombshell. Prescott had been playing a game I hadn't seen. I had to move, but what I'd learned held me still.

The results party buzzed with energy. Laughter echoed from every corner, glasses clinked, and people hovered around the TV screens, showing the election returns. I tried to smile.

I entered the room, heads turned, and a few people waved me over. "Breanna, you made it!" someone shouted, their voices full of excitement. I nodded and smiled, but my mind was on Ashley's confession.

Aaron stood near the front, his back to me, eyes locked on the returns. The numbers were in his favor for now, and the room hummed with the optimism that comes before the fall. His team gathered around him, joking, their faces lit with hope. I walked over to him, catching his eye.

"How's it looking?" I asked.

"We're ahead," he said, his eyes flashing between excitement and relief. "If the numbers keep up, this might happen."

I tried to match his smile, but it didn't reach my eyes. Aaron noticed. His expression softened as he looked at me. "What happened at the hospital?" His voice dropped.

"We need to talk," I said. I took his arm and guided him toward the corner, away from the crowd.

"We were alone," I told him. "Ashley's connected to Prescott. She helped him years ago."

Aaron's face darkened. "What? How?"

"She didn't understand at first, but she was part of one of his early schemes," I said. "It wasn't by choice, but she covered for him. She thought she fixed it by working with us here."

Aaron ran a hand through his hair, stepping back as he processed the news. "Why didn't she tell us sooner?"

"She felt scared," I said. "She thought she'd lose everything."

He stared at the ground, his jaw clenched. "We're too close to this election to be blindsided like this. Can we trust her now?"

"I don't know," I said. "There's more. Prescott isn't who we thought. He's Fredrick's son. The man we put away."

He froze, his hands at his sides. "Fredrick's son?"

I nodded. "He changed his name. This entire campaign has been about revenge. He's been after us from the start."

Aaron's face hardened, his eyes narrowing. "So this was never about politics."

"No," I said, shaking my head. "It's personal."

He stood silent for a moment, the noise of the party fading around us. "We need to be ready for whatever comes next."

The joy in the room felt distant now, as if it didn't belong to us. Aaron turned back toward the crowd, his shoulders stiffening.

"We still have tonight," he said, his voice quieter. "I don't think this fight ends with the election."

Aaron's eyes were still on the numbers when I said, "There's something I didn't realize about Olivia."

He glanced over, confusion creasing his brow. "What about her?"

"She's Ashley's daughter," I said. The words felt heavier than I expected. "She has known all along."

His face shifted in surprise. "Wait, she knew? You didn't?"

I shook my head. "No, I didn't. I found out at the hospital. Ashley told me."

Aaron stood there, absorbing it. "Olivia's been keeping this from you the whole time?"

"She wasn't hiding it," I said. "She never brought it up. She didn't think it mattered what we were doing here. Olivia kept their connection quiet, but she always understood who her mother was. They left me in the dark.

His expression tightened. "So, she's been dealing with all this behind the scenes."

I sighed. "No. And now it makes sense. She was protecting her, keeping her out of Prescott's mess."

Aaron's jaw clenched.

"She's been in this longer than I realized," I said. "She's smart. She knows what's going on."

He stared out into the room, his eyes narrowing. "We need to ensure Prescott never finds out about this. He would have used her connection to Ashley against us.

"I agree," I said. "We need to be careful, but Olivia's stronger than we think."

His face stayed hard. "I don't want her getting pulled any deeper into this. We've got to keep her out of Prescott's sights."

"I'll watch out for her," I said. "She's already in this. She understands more than we thought."

Time dragged on, and the energy in the room shifted. What had started as hopeful chatter was now replaced by quiet conversations. Aaron's lead, once solid, shrank. The numbers on the screen told the story we didn't want to believe.

I stood by the wall, arms crossed, watching the gap between Aaron and Brooks close. Every update hit like a punch to the gut. People around us were whispering. I caught his eye across the room.

"They're catching up," Thomas said. He stared at his tablet. "He is gaining."

Aaron stopped pacing, running a hand through his hair. "How bad is it?"

"We're trailing by a couple hundred votes. It's close."

His face hardened, but he said nothing. He looked toward the TV, watching as the final precincts reported. Supporters gathered in small groups, their earlier excitement replaced by tense glances and murmurs.

I moved closer to him, standing beside him. "We're still in this," I said, though the numbers told me otherwise.

He glanced at me, his expression tired. "It's slipping, Breanna. We're losing ground fast."

We both turned toward the screen. The last votes were being counted. The results were coming in, but the gap had grown. He had pulled ahead.

The room became hushed as the tally appeared. Brooks had won. By a slim margin, enough to take it. The silence stretched, broken only by the shuffling of feet and whispered curses.

Aaron stood frozen. His shoulders slumped. "We lost," he said.

I didn't realize what to say. There was no comfort in words, no way to soften the blow. I placed a hand on his arm.

The campaign team huddled near the front, some staring at the numbers, others shaking their heads in disbelief. A few tried to offer encouraging words, but they sounded hollow.

Thomas approached Aaron, his expression tight. "We came close."

His eyes are still on the screen. "Not close enough."

The air in the room grew heavier. Supporters trickled out, offering pats on the back and murmuring their regrets. The victory within reach was gone, slipping through our fingers in the last moments.

He sighed, turning to me. "I guess this is it."

I stepped beside him, laying a hand on his shoulder. The numbers were still on the screen, blinking like a reminder of what had slipped away. His head hung low, and I witnessed the tension in his body, the way his jaw clenched. I wanted to say something and offer comfort, but every word was empty before it left my lips.

"It was so close," I said, knowing it wouldn't help.

Aaron shook his head, more in acceptance than denial. "It doesn't matter. We lost." His voice was steady, but its weight cut through me. He wasn't angry, resigned. It was the defeat that lingered.

People remaining in the room started gathering around him. They patted his back and murmured their support. I watched as they said one by one, "You gave it everything," "We were right there." The smiles they forced were thin, fading as soon as they stepped away. The excitement, the hope that had filled this room earlier in the night, was gone.

"This isn't the end." Breaking the silence. Aaron's voice was quiet, but it carried across the room. "We lost tonight, but I'm not done fighting for this town."

He looked at me, and for a moment, I spotted a flicker of something in his eyes—not hoped, but resolve. "There are other ways to make a difference. Politics isn't the only path."

I nodded, experiencing the ache in my chest as I watched him gather himself. "You're not walking away from this," I said. It wasn't a question.

Aaron squared his shoulders, standing a little taller despite the weight of the loss still pressing down. "I'm not. There's still work to do."

The surrounding team took a little comfort in that. There were nods and small murmurs of agreement, but the room remained somber. The sting of the loss wouldn't fade tonight.

I stepped back as he talked to his team, already thinking ahead. He had a quiet strength now, something I hadn't seen before. In defeat, he wasn't backing down. My heart ached for him, knowing how much this meant and how close we'd come.

I experienced a deep pride. It's not over. Not for him. Not for us.

"We'll find a way," he said, his eyes meeting mine again. I believed him. The loss was actual, but so was his determination.

I watched him as he stood there, his shoulders squared. There was something steady and unshaken as defeat lingered in the air. He didn't complain or make excuses. He accepted it and kept moving forward while we still processed the sting.

I admired that about him—how he stood firm when everything crumbled. He had lost but not broken. That kind of strength wasn't loud or boastful.

He turned toward me, catching my eye. "We'll be fine," he said, his voice calm, like he already realized we would be.

I nodded, sensing my chest tighten. "I know. You always find a way."

Aaron gave a small smile that didn't need words. His eyes held mine for a moment, and in that silence, I could sense his resolve and commitment to this town, to the people, and to me. He wasn't fighting for himself. He focused on something bigger.

I reached out and touched his arm, detecting the tension still there, but beneath it, there was strength.

Aaron's eyes softened, and he placed his hand over mine. "I love you. More than this campaign, more than any of this."

The room was still buzzing with quiet conversations, people lingering as they processed the results. "You're going to make a difference," I said. "You already have."

He nodded, and I grasped he believed it. The loss hadn't shaken him. It had only strengthened him. I loved him more for it.

Chapter 11

The following day, the house was quiet. Aaron sat at the kitchen table, flipping through the paper, though he was not reading. I could tell by how his eyes moved over the page without focus.

I poured coffee, set two mugs down, and joined him. The smell of bacon filled the room, and the soft clatter of plates brought a sense of normalcy.

"Eggs, alright?" I asked, pushing his plate toward him.

He glanced up, managing a smile. "Perfect."

We ate for a while, the warmth of the coffee cutting through the early morning chill. I observed Aaron taking his time with every bite, lost in thought.

His face was calm, but he was still working through everything. "I've been thinking," finally breaking the silence.

I raised an eyebrow, taking a sip. "About what?"

He leaned forward, resting his elbows on his knees. "I'm not done," he said, his voice calm. "I don't think I can walk away."

I nodded, watching him. "You're considering running again?"

He looked at me, and I saw the determination in his eyes. "Maybe not right away. Yeah, I'm not ruling it out."

I sensed the possibility in his words. "What do we do?" I asked, shifting closer.

He thought for a moment and met my gaze. "We rebuild. Focus on the community. Start small. Engage people involved in something that matters."

I smiled. "That's what you're good at. Bringing people together."

He shrugged, but I realized he took the compliment. "I've been thinking...we set up some initiatives...work on what the campaign couldn't finish."

I rested my hand on his arm. "I'm with you. Whatever you want to do, I'm here."

He turned his head, a small smile playing at the corners of his mouth. "You are, aren't you? Every step."

I nodded. "I believe in you, Aaron. More than anything."

He took my hand, squeezing it. "I couldn't have gotten through this without you. You understand that, right?"

"I couldn't imagine doing it with anyone else."

We sat there, our hands intertwined, reflecting on everything we had been through. The loss had stung, but it hadn't broken us. It had strengthened us.

He looked ahead, his eyes clear. "We'll be ready."

I smiled, knowing he meant it. "Next time, we win."

I drove to the hospital with a heavy heart. The last few days had been a whirlwind, and now I needed to face Ashley. Her confession had left me reeling with each passing minute.

The lobby was a blur of muted colors and hushed voices. I walked to the elevator, my footsteps echoing in the quiet space. I reached Ashley's room. I paused outside the door. Taking a deep breath, I pushed it open.

She laid in bed, her face pale and tired. The room was lit, and her breathing was slow. Olivia sat beside her, holding her hand.

"Hey," I step inside.

Her eyes flickered open. She gave a weak smile. "Breanna..."

I pulled up a chair. "I wanted to find out how you're doing."

Her gaze shifted to Olivia, who patted her mother's hand. "She's been amazing," she said, her voice above a whisper. "I understand this is hard."

I nodded. "Your role in all this, it changes things."

Ashley took a deep breath, struggling to speak. "I was... involved before I even discovered. I didn't want to hurt anyone."

I reached out, touching her hand. "It's all so complicated."

She squeezed my hand, her eyes earnest. "No matter what... keep fighting for the truth."

A lump formed in my throat. I saw the strain in her eyes, the burden she carried. "I will. I promise."

She nodded, her eyes closing as if she were gathering her strength. Olivia wiped a tear from her cheek, watching us with concern and resignation.

"Thank you," I stood up. "For everything."

Ashley's hand fell to the side, and she gave me one last faint smile. I left the room, acknowledging the gravity of the journey.

The drive home was a blur of streetlights and shadows. I fought to keep my emotions in check, focusing on the road ahead. Each street sign and turn blurred into the next.

A lump formed in my throat as I gripped the steering wheel tighter. A relationship that began in competition had grown into something much deeper. Ashley had become a friend, and her health was now a source of immense concern. The drive seemed endless, as if I were moving through a thick fog of emotion.

I pulled into the driveway and entered the house, the silence heavy. I settled in, and my phone rang. The caller ID displayed Ashley's number, and my heart sank. I hesitated before answering, my fingers trembling.

"Hello?"

A choked sob came through the line. "Breanna, it's Olivia. I'm so sorry. Mom... she passed away after you left."

My breath caught in my throat. "No, Olivia, I... I'm so sorry."

Olivia's voice was audible. "I wanted you to know. Mom said you were a good friend."

Tears streamed down my face, mingling with my silent breaths. "Thank you for calling. I wish I had been there."

She whispered. "She appreciated your support."

I wiped my eyes, trying to compose myself. "Please, if I can do anything, please reach out to me. I am here for you."

The call ended, leaving me alone with my thoughts. I sat down on the couch, staring at the empty room. Ashley's death felt like a gaping wound, one that would take time to heal. Her last words, urging me to keep fighting, echoed in my mind.

The fight now was a tribute to the friend I had lost. The evening was dark, but I resolved to honor her memory by continuing the battle she had believed in.

I took a deep breath and dialed the Station Manager, Connie. The phone rang a few times before she answered.

"It's Breanna," I said, trembling. "I need to talk to you about Ashley."

There was a pause, and I sensed concern. "What's going on?"

I swallowed hard. "She passed away after I left the hospital."

"Oh," Connie's voice was soft, filled with sorrow. "I'm so sorry to discover that."

"I want to honor her. Despite her brief time with us, her impact was significant. I want to dedicate a tribute to her work at the station."

Connie was quiet for a moment. "I think that's a wonderful idea. She made a difference here in her short duration. I'll put you in charge of organizing it."

Relief washed over me. "Thank you. I want to remember her contributions.

"Of course. I'll alert the rest of the team about her passing," Connie said. "Everyone will want to contribute."

We exchanged a few more words, and I ended the call. I wanted to honor that fight by celebrating her memory. I listed what needed to be done.

I found Aaron in the living room, staring out the window as if trying to peer through the fog. My steps weighed heavily as I approached him.

"I got off the phone with Connie. Ashley... she passed away."

His head turned, confusion clouding his eyes. "What? When?"

"After I left the hospital," I said before my composure broke. I sank into the couch beside him, tears streaming down my face.

Aaron's eyes filled with empathy as he reached out and drew me close. His arms encircled me, a firm anchor in the storm of my grief. I let out ragged sobs, my breaths coming in sharp, uneven bursts.

"Aaron, I feel like I should have done more."

"Shh," he murmured, his voice unwavering. "You did everything you could. Ashley understood you cared."

He rubbed my back - a silent comfort. I felt his heart beating against my cheek. Despite the ache in my chest, his presence offered a strange solace. My hands clutched his shirt, seeking something solid during my turmoil.

"I keep thinking about Olivia," I said. "How will she cope with this?"

Aaron's grip tightened. "She's strong, like her mother. It's going to be difficult. We need to be there for her."

I nodded, trying to absorb his words. The room appeared small and suffocating, with the enormity of the loss pressing in from all sides. I leaned into Aaron, letting the warmth of his embrace seep into my cold, trembling body.

"I didn't expect this to hit so hard," I admitted. "Ashley was making a difference."

"I understand. It's unfair. We can honor her memory by continuing the fight."

My tears slowed, though the ache in my chest remained. I took a deep breath, pulling back to look at him. "What do we do now?"

He wiped a stray tear from my cheek with his thumb. "We remember what she stood for. We keep pushing forward, no matter how it gets."

I tried to smile, the effort bringing a faint glimmer of hope amidst the grief. "You're right. We owe it to her."

He nodded, his expression firm but filled with compassion. "We'll make it through this. Together."

The phone rang, slicing through the silence. I pulled away from him, wiping my tears. With shaky hands, I picked up the receiver.

The sound cut through the quiet, pulling me back to the present. He looked up from the couch, his eyes catching mine as I answered it. I didn't recognize the number, but something told me to answer.

"Breanna, there's something you need to realize. Prescott's not the only one involved. This goes deeper."

My heart skipped, a chill running down my spine. "Who is this?"

The line crackled in silence. I stood frozen, the words echoing in my mind.

Aaron looked at me. "What's going on?"

I set the phone down, my thoughts racing. "Someone called. They said Prescott was not at the end. There's more. It's bigger than we thought."

Aaron didn't flinch. His eyes locked onto mine, the same calm strength I relied on. "We'll figure it out."

I nodded. We had faced the trials before, and we had made it through. Whatever came next, I recognized we could handle it.

Aaron stood, pulling me into a tight embrace. "We'll keep fighting," his lips brushing my forehead. "Together."

I leaned into him, closing my eyes. "Together," I repeated.

Acknowledgements

Writing a book is never a solitary endeavor, and I am profoundly grateful to the remarkable individuals who shaped *Pursuing Justice* into what it is today.

First, a heartfelt thank you to Amanda R, Sara Davil, Tiffany Vega, and Jess B. Your insights, feedback, and relentless dedication to refining this story have been invaluable. Your commitment to this project has made all the difference, and I sincerely appreciate your contributions.

To my daughter Breanna. It haws been a joy for me to watch you develop into the fine woman you have become.

Lastly, a huge thank you to my readers. Your willingness to embark on this journey with me means more than I can express. I hope you find something in these pages that resonates with you, and my greatest wish is that you see a part of yourself in the character of Holli.

The next installment of this story will be released in the spring of 2026. Join our community and stay updated by signing up at www.hojopresspublishing.com

About the Author

John Russell is a seasoned author and expert in organizational leadership, having earned his doctorate from National University. He is the author of the acclaimed four-book Published Investigation series. He has recently expanded his literary portfolio with Stories from the Heart, a collection of five compelling short stories.

The Investigation series, inspired by John's wife and three grown daughters, began as a heartfelt Christmas gift to them, reflecting his dedication to both family and storytelling. His entrepreneurial spirit led him to establish HojoPress Publishing in December 2023, where he continues to craft and share stories that resonate with readers.

John's life is rich with personal passions beyond writing. He is an avid sports enthusiast and finds joy in his family life. He is married with three daughters and two grandchildren, and he cherishes the companionship of his basset hound. John embodies a life of creativity, leadership, and connection through his work and hobbies.

Books From John Russell

<u>Investigation Series</u>
Friendship Unveiled
The Heroes of Centerville
Kodiak Mysteries
Clarkston Secrets

<u>Holli Series</u>
Pursuing Justice

<u>Breanna Series</u>
Behind the Headlines

Other Books from John Russell
Stories from the Heart
Love Songs (Spring 2025)

Be sure to follow John Russell at: Goodreads.com; BookBub.com & LinkedIn for more update on future projects and behind the scenes content.

Purchase these from:

Amazon.com

BN.com

Apple Books

Kobo.com

www.hojopresspublishing.com

www.ingramcontent.com/pod-product-compliance
Lightning Source LLC
Chambersburg PA
CBHW060509030426
42337CB00015B/1821